The message of *Tales from the*  and inspiring as John Doyle invites the reader to come along and catch the spirit of the ups and downs of the aging process. After turning to the first page I just couldn't put it down. The author shares a memorable story replete with fascinating experiences and personal insights. His humor and pathos are truly infectious.

Father James Hawker,
Former Pastor, (retired)
Quincy, Mass.

I am greatly impressed with both the clarity of the writing and the truthfulness of this book. John Doyle speaks out openly, freely and honestly about many things concerning the aging process that others may think about but cannot put into words.

Iris Devore
Founder of Levine Senior Center
Matthews, NC

Many books offer advice on selecting a retirement community, but what about life inside the community once the decision has been made? With humor and the wisdom of his 88 years the author tells us stories of the new, rich and sometimes frustrating life that he and his wife experience in their new home.

George Mundle, PhD.
Executive Director
Charlotte-Mecklenburg Council on Aging (retired)

TALES
FROM THE
TAIL END

TALES FROM THE TAIL END

iUniverse books may be ordered through booksellers or by contacting:

iUniverse
1663 Liberty Drive
Bloomington, IN 47403
www.iuniverse.com
1-800-Authors (1-800-288-4677)

ISBN: 978-1-4502-5535-6 (pbk)
ISBN: 978-1-4502-5536-3 (ebk)

Printed in the United States of America

iUniverse rev. date: 9/20/2010

TALES
FROM THE
TAIL END

What old people know about aging that no
gerontologist can ever know —as told from an
elderly retirement community.

John V. Doyle

iUniverse, Inc.

New York   Bloomington

All the people in this book (except the author and his family) have been given fictitious first names only. The name of the retirement community where the author and his wife reside is also fictitious (and original with rights available).

The purpose of this device, as everyone knows, is to protect the innocent from being confused with the guilty. Good enough, but I have thought everyone in this book to be innocent.

To all our dear friends at Haven Lake
who wear their crowns most jauntily.

"If old age means a crown of thorns,
the trick is to wear it jauntily."

Clare Booth Luce

Gerontology (from the Greek, *geron,* "old man" and
–ology, "study of"), is the study of the social, psychological
and biological aspects of aging. It is distinguished from
geriatrics, which is the branch of medicine that studies the
disease of aging.

Chapters

Introduction

A sense of humor is often the only antidote for the many trials and tribulations that define the aging process. Thus I hope readers will find and happily share a chuckle or two as they hear about — or come to anticipate — the grim realities of their own tail end tales.

Another necessity for survival is the knowledge of what to expect. Therefore, I have been fully outspoken about the sufferings and trials that can assault us as the years add up. In turn, I hope I have also revealed some things that can be done to deal with them or to simply cope if that becomes necessary.

My case has been made within the environment of an independent living retirement community just because my wife and I have chosen that course for our own latter years. But other possible courses have been reviewed and are equally deserving of consideration. Whatever course you might decide to take, the experiences will be much the same.

Seek expert advice and investigate different choices before you and/or your family make final decisions for living out your last days. Speak to the managers of retirement communities of all types. If you find managers and an environment that appeal to you, try them out. Request the opportunity to live with them for a few days or a week. Some places might offer this privilege at no charge if you present yourself as a very likely new resident.

But no amount of investigation can prepare one for the actual experience. It is for that reason that I offer these very true tales from the tail end of life as they are lived here and now by my wife and me and many dear friends in a place called Haven Lake.

1.
The facts of elderly life.

Elderly people — over 80 that is —know something totally, yes totally, unknown to any other people. They know what it is like to grow old. Doctors may have dens wallpapered with degrees in geriatrics, but they don't know. Statisticians may have filing cabinets stuffed with survey results, but they don't know. Managers of retirement communities may have great devotion for us, but even they don't know. Children, especially children, do not understand the aging of their parents. Their perception is obscured by love, expectation and fear. What it is like to grow old cannot be taught. It cannot be learned. As younger people often assume, it cannot even be imagined. To be known, aging must be lived.

This truism can frustrate, aggravate and, fortunately, sometimes greatly amuse the elderly. When we (the author is 88) get together to exchange feelings, experiences, hopes, fears, or whatever might befuddle our doddering old heads, the unknowingness of younger people often dominates the discussion, which usually reaches this conclusion: Talking to *them* is useless.

Then why write about old age, as this book proposes to do? Because, like Mount Everest, it is there! Although readers under 80 may not reach any summit of sensitivity by reading this book, one can hope they will be inspired to anticipate rather than fear or shut from mind that time when they, too, might plant the flag atop the crest and, along with those of us now there, take glory in that achievement.

It is just because old age is a glorious achievement that this book is being written — primarily for the enjoyment, the satisfaction and most surely the recognition of the elderly. All others, especially children and grandchildren, are invited to look over our shoulders to scoff, sympathize or chuckle, as they see fit. Indeed, they would be well advised to do so. They need to know what life if like for their elderly loved ones. They need to remember that their time will come!

The author's original hope was to write a humorous book. The elderly do laugh a lot. It helps smother the distress of aging. But aging is serious stuff — not for sissies, as the repeated saying goes. Or, as my grandson John would say when he was a wee lad and I put some tease on him, "'Snot funny, grampa!" On the other hand, when he heard of this book project some twenty-five years later, same grandson said, "Keep it funny, grampa. Nobody wants to read about old people's problems." I will try to heed both admonitions, but must tell the truth, silly or sorry or sad.

This book is written with soulful awareness of the uncounted elderly who wither away their latter years in sacrilegious, uncared-for solitude in some kind of sanitarium or special needs nursing home, supported only by Medicaid. It is written with a weeping awareness of all those elderly who struggle to live out their lives in some kind of clung-to private residence, too often unknown, unloved, unaided, supported only by Medicare. But this is neither of those stories. These tales are drawn from the growing ranks of elderly who, blessed with some kind of reasonable, still manageable health and wealth have chosen to live out their years in the active, caring, serving environment of a retirement community — any one of which is an incredible laboratory for researching the psyches of the elderly.

2.
Comes the time.

You are born. You are educated. You fall in love. You get a job. You get married. You raise a family. You build a career. You retire. For most people this is the fairly normal routine of life. Throughout all of it, the thing you think about least of all, if at all, is getting old. Then comes the year, the day, the hour when the truth hits you like a punch in the solar plexus. The signs, the sensations, the symptoms can no longer be denied. You are old!

Like it or not, ready or not, most everything in your life — and the lives of those who love you — changes at that point. How to cope, how to manage, how to live with this new, strange, often frightening change of life is a challenge beyond imagination.

My wife and I chose to meet that challenge by moving into Haven Lake, an independent living retirement community located in Charlotte, NC. Come join us there — for the truth about aging, for a good laugh, perhaps a tear or two, maybe even now and then a fit of anger.

3.
Mitzapuny soup.

In Haven Lake the monthly rent includes three meals a day. The dining room is the center of a social life highly concentrated on food. What is the menu for the day? Will each dish be well prepared? How will it taste? Too spicy? Too bland? Too regional? Not regional enough? (Located in the south, we have residents who are both natives and "come-heres."). Too caloric? Too sweet? (Most residents are on some kind of diet.) In short, the dining room is a forum for discussion of the culinary arts. Such discussions are, in fact, one of the unique and significant aspects of retirement community life. You may find this hard to believe and so did we. But it is the fact! From some necessity, we also try to keep it fun.

Our community management provides the agenda for this fascinating discourse. At every Sunday breakfast, a complete menu for the succeeding week is issued and snatched up faster and with more interest than the Sunday funnies. Also, the menu for each individual day is displayed in a plastic holder on every dining room table.

And there it was — Mitzapuny soup!

The three daily meals are breakfast served at 8:00 AM, dinner (the main meal) served at 12:30 PM and supper (a light meal) served at 5:30 PM. Supper routinely begins with a cup of soup — this evening Mitzapuny soup. The huge dining room (maximum seating capacity 144) buzzed with the question, "What is Mitzapuny soup?" At our table for four, I told our usual dining companions, Ramona and Fred, "I looked it up on the Internet. The Food Network never heard of it. The Cooking Network never heard of it. Mitzapuny soup is not to be found anywhere on the Internet." Throughout the dining room, anticipation, curiosity and not a little concern were palpable.

Now it happens that Jacob, our chief chef, habitually saunters out of his kitchen domain at every meal just before the servers do their job, grabs a portable mike, struts up and down the aisles between tables and repeats what we have just read on the menu about what he has prepared for us to eat. It is his moment to boast. At a chef/residents meeting he informed us that all menus, including recipes, are prepared — prescribed in fact — by a team of "culinary and dietary experts" in the home office of the community developer. With some bravado, he advises that he has no qualms about making slight departures from that prescription if he finds good reason. That reason might be the availability of some fresh, seasonal ingredient he can purchase locally rather than use the normal bulk deliveries of a major food distributor. Just as often, he says, chin jutting and arms akimbo, he simply decides to do something different. We came to fear this boast. More often than not, that "something different" suited his personal convenience and/or liking more than ours.

On the day in question, armed with this general knowledge, the entire dining room turned rapt attention to the kitchen's "Out" door awaiting Jacob's appearance — and a description of Mitzapuny Soup! But the mystery remains.

"Our soup tonight," he announced, "will be vegetable beef." No explanation of the weird name or menu change was offered. And, shame to say, not a single resident dared to ask, "So what the heck is Mitzapuny soup?" So now and maybe forever, whenever some food service displeases or puzzles us, our rallying cry will be — like "Remember the Maine" — "Remember the Mitzapuny soup!"

Gabby Crabby soup briefly threatened to dethrone Mitzapuny as the oddest ever menu item but couldn't cut it. Gabby Crabby contained a clue, at least. Mitzapuny means absolutely nothing!

If this silly episode suggests that our community residents attach great significance to and yet have reservations about the quality of the food served three times a day, it is justified. Despite all the activities offered for our participation and enjoyment, eating is still the major event. It is the one event in which all residents participate. It is the one experience that gives us a common ground for expressing our likes and dislikes. Most all agree that the dining experience can, to a large extent, determine the degree of happiness and satisfaction — or lack of it — we experience in this place where we have chosen to live out our last days on earth.

Needless to say, there will be more tales to tell about food!

Which simply begs the more important question: If life in a retirement community is so "iffy," why and how does one get there in the first place?

4.
Decisions, decisions!

This is not a how-to book. The object is to tell it like it is. But if there can be any doubt about the wisdom of choosing to live in a retirement community, the question must be asked, "Whatever drove us here in the first place?" A discussion of how it all happens is in order.

Many people approach the idea of moving to a retirement community with this question, "Where should we go?" But that is not the first consideration. First, you've got to decide you *need* to go. And that can be complicated. The vast majority of retirement communities fall within three categories:

1. Independent living with no medical facilities or services;

2. Independent living with some medical facilities and services available;

3. Total life care.

If you are really sick or senile or unable to care for yourself, it's too late for the first two categories. To get into either one of them you have to pass a physical investigation — it might be just a good hard look and interrogation — that indicates you can live independently upon entering the community.

If you get sick or physically frail in a category one facility you will be transported to a doctor or hospital. If you get sick in a category two facility, doctors, nurses and medical facilities of varying extents and capabilities are available on site, usually for increased fees. If you are not restored to reasonable good health in either of these facilities, you will be required to remove yourself to category three, a total care nursing home.

Independent living implies some remaining ability to perform normal personal care activities. Bathe. Dress. Take proper medications. Socialize. Get to the dining room and eat! And it commands the ability to properly behave. The Residency Agreement for our community states this in part as bluntly as this:

"Ending your occupancy may be appropriate if your actions or behaviors indicate that you (1) present a foreseeable direct threat to the health or safety of other individuals, (2) are likely to cause substantial physical damage to the property of the community or others, or (3) otherwise fail to abide by the Community's reasonable occupancy rules or this Agreement."

The Agreement is six pages long. The Occupancy Rules, other Addendums to the Agreement and a New Resident Handbook constitute another two dozen or more pages.

The three categories of care differ significantly in respect to costs.

Independent living facilities usually charge a modest entrance fee (like a month's rent) then a month by month rental charge. Usually, there is not even a lease to sign. You can pack up and leave any time you wish with few or no restrictions.

Independent living facilities with medical services charge a significant up-front entrance fee — like $200,000-plus! This is justified as a subsidy or endowment to be used to pay for the medical services if and when you need them. In rare cases, this fee is refunded to you if you leave or to your estate if you die. In most cases, there is no refund of this fee under any conditions. (One company's financial difficulty has raised questions about the wisdom of investing in these huge upfront fees. Will they actually be refundable?)

If an elderly person and his or her family members are not totally put off by this avalanche of caveats, qualifications and costs, chances are good that you really do *need* to make such a move. You might need to do it for any one or more of several reasons:

For a husband, it is usually being fed up with or becoming unable to perform the management responsibilities of a formal residence, such as a private home or condominium.

For a wife, it is usually being fed up with or becoming unable to perform the never-ending chores of cooking and housekeeping.

For a single person, male or female, it can be both of these plus a crushing need for some kind of social life and companionship.

For all those elderly who have lost or face the loss of driving privileges, it offers a variety of activities from which one can pick and choose and take up — in house!

For some it becomes emotionally and/or economically wise. Many elderly people, singles or couples, slowly, reluctantly come to realize that they are living in a big, empty house that was once a family home. Suddenly it is filled with no more than fading memories, loneliness and problems. Sure, the mortgage might be paid, but the home value has ballooned and so have the real estate taxes, utilities and repair costs. Excellent retirement communities are not economical living, but in some circumstances, when the plusses and minuses are tallied, cost savings can be possible.

Elderly who opt for an independent living facility are often asked this very good question: If you become physically unable to maintain the residency requirements, what happens then? The only answer is this: Until that time comes — if ever — you cannot know what needs to happen.

Why and how you lose your independence will determine your next step. Lessened physical abilities can often be replaced and/or managed by hiring in-house caretakers. Many excellent services of this sort are available. Independent living retirement communities welcome such service people and cooperate fully with those who receive such care. The cost can be high but will probably still be much less than the initial registration fees and ongoing charges you must pay to live in a facility that offers on-site health care, which must be subsidized and may never be needed.

Doctors and hospitals are almost always as readily accessible from an independent living facility as they are from a full service facility. Haven Lake is just a ten minute drive from an excellent major medical complex. If needed, transportation is provided and included in our rent.

The most feared eventuality is, of course, the nursing home. This observation is not meant to disparage nursing homes. With few exceptions, they are excellent, reputable, trustworthy facilities affording excellent care. But the simple fact remains that you go there as a last resort. Fortunately, the odds of that ever happening are very low. Less than 5% of the elderly spend their last days in a nursing home. And the average stay is but a few weeks.

Deciding how and where to manage your latter years can be a gamble. But so is crossing the street and driving a car. Since you've already made it into your eighties, why worry about a little extra risk in return for a little better life?

Having fully considered all of the above, with counsel from family members, friends, clergy, financial advisers, real estate agents and more, after endless soul searching, you make the momentous decision to end the kind of life you've lived for over 80 years or more and commit — yes, commit — to a totally new life in a retirement community. And then it really gets tough.

You've got a house to sell in a grossly depressed market (as this is written). You've got a lifetime collection of possessions — furnishings, clothing, memorabilia, precious personal treasures — to thin out, downsize or simply get rid of. As you tackle all of this, you ask yourself every day, every hour: "Have I lost my mind? How can I do all this? Why am I even trying to do it?" And because you've done your homework, the answer keeps coming back, "Because I need to."

Fortunately, different kinds of help are available to guide and assist you through this terribly trying time. Most often, children are your principal saviors. In the early, filling-up months of our retirement community, scarcely a day went by when we did not see some extended family — grandparents, parents, sons and daughters, grandchildren, sometimes siblings — seated in the dining room getting a "taste" of retirement living and what our community in particular offers. And when the decision was made and moving-in time came, the same family members could be seen assisting and supporting, physically and emotionally, their bewildered but beloved elders.

Professionals offer many services to help get the job done. Selling the old home. Helping decide what you need to keep in what will surely be a vastly smaller living space. Disposing of all the "stuff" you no longer need. Making the physical move.

Beware of these services. Before you engage them, know what you've got (do an inventory), know what it is worth (get an appraisal), and know the reputation and record of the parties offering any moving and, especially, downsizing services such as (1) home and yard sales, (2) used furniture and second-time-around outlets, (3) auctions, (4) charitable contributions.

Much of the disposition and moving task can be do-it-yourself. The most satisfying of all is giving to family and friends. Our three children and their spouses and three grandchildren had first "dibs" on anything in our house they wanted that we did not plan to take with us into the retirement community apartment. It gave us great joy to see the majority of our most prized possessions, no longer needed by us, find continuing love, care and respect from dear ones.

We consigned a number of our remaining finer items — furniture and artwork — to a reputable auction house where they found appreciative buyers and provided a very satisfying financial return.

Two or three weeks before we were scheduled to move in, the very considerate managers of Haven Lake gave us a key to the apartment. Day after day, I drove the ten mile round-trip from our house to the apartment with carloads of clothes, paintings, small furnishings, bedding — just about anything I could handle on my own.

We then engaged a well-recommended professional to finish the job. Our house was sold. The professional offered us a total deal — pack and move all that we would take with us, conduct an in-home estate sale, dispose of any remaining possessions to worthy charities, provide tax deductible receipts, and clean-up the empty premises to make them suitable for possession by the buyers. A packing and moving estimate was provided. It was agreed that proceeds from the estate sale would be applied towards the moving costs. A modest deposit was made to seal the deal. What a relief it was to dump all of this travail on someone else's shoulders.

So much for the mechanics of the momentous move. The reality of how it all comes about and how it actually plays out can be something else, as will be revealed with the tale of our own personal experience. Elderly readers will relate. All others may consider themselves properly alerted.

5.
Blame it on I-95!

My wife Fran and I retired to Florida in 1980. I did, that is. Her role as homemaker, social director, keeper of dates to be remembered and observed continued unabated for another 30 years — until we moved into the retirement community, of course.

The Florida move perpetuated a family Diaspora begun when our three children first went off to college. Yet we are a remarkably close, loving family needing regular doses of togetherness with our three children and three grandchildren. Daughter Kathleen and husband Phill then lived in Arlington, VA. Daughter Ginny and husband Bill lived in Charlotte, NC. Son Fred and wife Mary lived in Alexandria, VA. All had jobs to keep them busy, families to rear — and excuses galore for not travelling to Florida. It became our job to do most of the visiting to and fro.

Hello I-95! Hello I-40! Hello I-77! I-95 became the monster.

After about the thirtieth trip up north and back (at least three a year for ten years) I-95 bored us beyond belief and beleaguered us with ever heavier traffic the closer we came to DC. Speed ceased to be an object. Relief was sought on any other route, indeed *every* other route that would get us off I-95 yet to our destination. Route 17, the original, fascinating east coast highway. Route 1, honky-tonk town almost all the way. Route 321, rural and historical. We drove them all, all the way, many times to inevitable ennui.

Otherwise, our eighteen years in Florida were good. Stuart on the east coast, 100 miles above Miami, half way between Palm Beach and Vero Beach, was a delightful place to live. (Not so much any more.) As members of the Newcomers Club, we made many friends easily, delightfully. We golfed and bowled at least once a week. Fran was the Pearl Mesta of our group, entertaining frequently, graciously, deliciously in our roomy home. We travelled extensively in the U.S. and abroad. We had the pool, the boat, the whole magilicutty!

These years were also deeply emotional and revealing about aging. I sat for many hours in shock and sorrow beside Bob, a very dear friend, watching him wither away and die from Alzheimer's disease. Shamefully, I now realize, I silently chastised my dearest friend, Dick, for complaining about the difficulty he had walking. "For Pete's sake, man," I thought, "you can stand. So just put one foot in front of the other and walk." But he was not the biblical cripple; I was not Jesus Christ. When he died shortly thereafter of heart failure, his widow requested and I delivered his eulogy. I portrayed him as the beloved curmudgeon he surely was. But if

I had known then what I know now about growing old, I would also have begged his forgiveness.

Eighteen years of this kind of life passed, but who was counting? We were just in our mid seventies and despite the death of too many dear friends we still felt immortal. It was our children who began to worry. Should we be doing all that travelling or, worse, all that driving "at our ages?" First there were hints, then insistence: We needed to think about moving north again, nearer to family care. After thorough consultation all around, it was decided in 1997 that our new home would be Williamsburg, VA. Much closer to all the children, but favoring none.

Williamsburg was good fun for almost six years. "Good Neighbor" passes, available to all city residents, gave us free entrance to all Colonial Williamsburg offerings, all within walking distance from our home. When we got our fill of all that, we spent many happy hours at sidewalk cafes in the historical district sipping coffee in the winter, iced tea in the summer, ogling the steady stream of tourists. Stuffed with the wisdom of our years, smug with the experience of long lives, we felt it quite our right to assess that cross section of America with this oft repeated, snarky observation: "And believe it or not, they all vote!"

But in time the new road to Charlotte, I-85, along with the remaining very worst stretch of I-95 to Washington DC renewed our discontent. Williamsburg had been a compromise. It did not end our Diaspora. Family visits were almost as difficult as before. Daughter Ginny in Charlotte, nurturing by nature, finally said, "Come see a new housing development here that I think you will love." Also by then, Kathleen had been widowed for many years and had retired from a most successful career with a DC publishing firm. She was hinting that she could easily be uprooted from the capital city area.

In 2003, we sold in Williamsburg and bought Ginny's recommended home in Charlotte. Shortly after we moved there, Kathleen sold her big home in Arlington and bought an uptown Charlotte condominium. Suddenly, finally, family togetherness had been restored by two-thirds.

Five years in that Charlotte home slowly but surely brought to the fore all the reasons people move into retirement communities. Another round of family consultations in 2007 decided that we should begin the search for a retirement community that would be right for us. Our first explorations were put-offs. Yes, we were now in our mid-eighties, but those places seemed filled with really old people! We were not ready for canes, walkers, wheelchairs.

And yet, every time an appliance failed just after the warranty expired, every time the property taxes and utility rates went up, every time there was a minor disaster in the kitchen, every time we forgot why we had just walked from one room to another, every time our doctors put us on a new pill, dissatisfaction, frustration and worry rose in tandem. The time had come to DO IT!

6.
Welcome to Haven Lake.

We paid a refundable deposit to get our name on the waiting list of a large retirement community in Matthews, NC. Their waiting time was as much as three years. We paid a refundable deposit to get on the charter residents list at a second community, also in Matthews. At the time it was no more than a sales center with construction scheduled to begin in late 2008. First occupancy was targeted for late 2009, a date no one really believed. Both offered independent living with medical facilities for extended care. All other establishments we considered were readily dismissed for one reason or another.

We were in limbo. The decision to do it had been made but there was no place for us to go for the foreseeable future. A sense of miserable frustration set in, exacerbating all the reasons for making the move. We began to wonder if we had waited too long. We feared we might not even live long enough to make the move. I began to physically ail and lose weight.

Once again, our daughter Ginny came to the rescue. "I've been searching some more and I've found the perfect place! It's just around the corner from us. It's under construction and almost finished. It will be ready in just a few months. You've got to see it." It was Haven Lake, an independent retirement living community on the east side of Charlotte.

In March, 2008, we met Haven Lake managers Geena and Adam. They toured and dined us at another newly completed, partially populated sister community in northeast Charlotte. While there, I put my arm around Geena and said, "You ... just ... might ... be ... our ... guardian ... angel!"

Compared to most other retirement communities, Haven Lake is a small facility with a total of only about 120 apartments. (Others are in the many hundreds.) We liked that. We could probably get to know every one of our neighbors. We selected apartment number 123, two bedrooms, two baths, and secured it with a deposit. We listed our house for sale and began making plans to move as soon as Haven Lake was ready for occupancy, then promised for October or November, 2008.

News media then bellowed: "Major recession under way!" Our assets plummeted. This made us wary about moving without first selling the house. Then the real estate market collapsed. I told Geena and Adam that our planned moving date was suddenly very iffy. All agreed to maintain the status quo with first refusal rights on the apartment we had reserved.

We had one early offer on the house, from a woman moving from Florida to be close to her children in Charlotte. (Sound familiar?) It was contingent on the sale of her home in Florida, where the housing market was in greater shambles than Charlotte.

No deal, advised our realtor. After six months of no further action, we finally decided that our listing had become stale and should be cancelled. If conditions improved in 2009, we would renew it. Our realtor agreed. The "For Sale" sign and literature box were removed from our property. Fran and I resigned ourselves to a long stay just where we were, like it or not! Adam and Geena were again most considerate and suggested that we keep our agreement with them just as it was, see what happened — and pray!

Prayers were answered. On a sunny day in January, 2009, while walking our beautiful beagle, Maggie, I noticed a car cruising our neighborhood. Lookers, I thought. Sure enough, they pulled into a driveway and took a flyer from a promo box there. (Six or seven units were still for sale in the community.) When the car drove out past Maggie and me, it stopped, a window rolled down and the driver said, "Hi."

"Hi. Are you shopping?" I asked.

"Yes we are. Can you tell us something about the community?"

"Certainly. But I see you have Florida license plates. Have you sold your property there?"

"Yes, we have."

"Let's talk," I said.

We sold them our house without a broker. Maggie earned the commission. We talked to Adam and Geena. The chosen apartment was still available. The wheels were set in motion for a March 1, 2009, move to Haven Lake.

As I reported earlier, we did much of the light moving ahead of time on our own. Then we hired the "professional" to do everything else. That would include the final moving job, conducting an in-house estate sale for everything not moved or otherwise disposed of, removing everything that remained unsold and cleaning the premises for new owner occupancy. It was agreed that all unsold items would be donated to worthy charities and receipts obtained for tax deductions.

Moving date was set for Thursday, February 27. Geena and Adam insisted that we should stay in the apartment Thursday, Friday and Saturday even though our first rental payment would be due Sunday March 1. Preparations for the estate sale were to be made on a Friday. The actual sale would take place on Saturday, beginning at 7:00 AM. I passed this word as far and wide as I could to help drum up action among friends and neighbors. We had a quantity of fine stuff to dispose of and were proud to offer it to one and all.

Moving was a mixed affair. The moving men were ill-trained klutzes who broke legs on three end tables (repaired by our talented son-in-law, Bill). But thanks to a floor plan I had drawn, all chosen furnishings for the Haven Lake apartment fit as if they had been designed for it.

The estate sale was a horror. When I came upon the scene Friday morning to check on the proceedings, I discovered that our service provider had driven a truck up our driveway, unloaded an assortment of stuff from her own resale establishment — and had begun the sale! I found her as busy selling her "junque" as she was our fine possessions. And as near as I could tell, she was making no separation of the proceeds. She was also trying to manage the entire sale on her own. When busy in the house, she had no idea what was happening in the garage or on the driveway or vise versa.

In either unattended area, thefts were an obvious possibility and probably a reality.

When I took her to task for this state of affairs, she became very defensive. "I know what I'm doing," she said. "My merchandise helps attract customers." This claim was so pathetic there was simply no rejoinder to be made. But it was too late to cancel. The turnout was very good. Sales were being made. We had to let things run their course.

On Saturday morning, friends and neighbors I had advised of the sale showed up only to learn with disappointment that much of the good stuff was sold on Friday. On the other hand, it rained hard on Saturday and the turnout was disappointing. The manager of the event found this a good reason to gloat about her wisdom in starting the sale a day early.

In fairness, the premises were left empty and very clean, as promised. But we received no receipts for the donation of unsold items to charity. We suspect that all those items wound up in the manager's resale establishment. But we had neither the will nor energy to investigate and try to make that case.

Pay back was achieved when it was all over and the time came to balance out charges and receipts. Daughter Ginny led the negotiation. For every charge assessed, she countered with a deduction for negligence, malfeasance or failure to perform as promised. When it was done we did not feel so totally taken.

We interrupt our tale at this point for a special news bulletin.

Mitzapuny soup redux!

The mystery soup is on the menu again! Feeling bold after almost five months of residency, I now seek to solve the mystery — whatever it takes, whomever it might embarrass. Co-manager Andrew is on duty. Before we eat, I challenge him to make the chef reveal precisely what it is we are going to be eating. But, as usual, the soup is served before the chef announces the main dish and we discover for ourselves that *this* Mitzapuny soup is basically lima beans and chunky ham. Quite delicious, in fact, but clearly *not* the vegetable beef of its first appearance. More the mystery.

New chef Caleb (not Jacob, another tale to come) then appears out of the kitchen and announces, "I have been asked to explain Mitzapuny soup. I cannot. It was named that in the menu that came from corporate headquarters. I've personally never heard of it. My guess is that it might be a variation of mulligatawny stew."

No way! We all know what mulligatawny stew is. Unsatisfied, I get recognized and ask, "Is this soup we have just eaten made from a corporate supplied recipe?"

"Yes, it is."

So we now know three things, at least. (1) Chef Jacob altered the recipe the first time, most likely to avoid just this kind of interrogation. (2) The mystery originated in corporate headquarters; our chefs are exonerated. (3) Unless the matter is referred to headquarters for explanation, which we do not contemplate as yet, our rallying cry shall remain, "Remember the Mitzapuny soup!"

Back to our tale. With the horrendous job of moving behind us, thankful for the best of it, trying to forget the worst of it, we dedicated our minds, hearts and efforts to the task of settling into the most unusual — one might say weird — living circumstances of our entire lives. We were certain our move to Haven Lake was necessary, but would it be a happy, satisfying, fulfilling experience for our remaining years? We had left ourselves no retreat. We were as much frightened as hopeful. Come along, dear reader, as the tumultuous tale continues.

7.

Is this seat taken?

Prior to our targeted Haven Lake move in date, Fran and I had dined there once or twice as guests of managers Geena and Adam. Of course we looked around each time to see what kind of people occupied the dining room. A couple of them stood out. Beautiful, brave Brenda, so dependent upon her walker. Magnificent Winslow, a 95-year old black man with a voice like a kettle drum roll. But we had no need at that time to make meaningful judgments about future neighbors.

All that changed March 1, 2009. We walked into that dining room totally aware that we were the new guys in town. The tables were turned. We were now getting the scrutiny. What we liked mattered not. The question was: Would we be liked? It was an unnerving experience. Yet we had to stand there, gawking like a pair of goony birds, looking for a place to sit, searching for a face or two that might welcome us.

There is no assigned seating at Haven Lake. (We soon learned from other residents that some retirement communities do have such a strange rule.) So we looked for vacant seats. The first blessing of our new life was found at a nearby table with two empty seats and two others occupied by Ramona and Fred. We sat with them. They greeted us warmly.

Picture the 1930 painting "American Gothic" by Grant Wood and you will see these two very dear people. Quiet. Unassuming. Interesting. Above all, welcoming. We vowed that day to make them our permanent dining partners — if they would have us. And they would. For the next several weeks we four ate at the very same table, cementing each day another brick in the foundation of our friendship.

Ours was not the only "reserved" table. Only forty or fifty people were in residence when we moved in and most of them had already found permanent dining partners. But when Cameron was hired as Haven Lake marketing manager, newcomers began arriving, one or two at first, then three or four in a row. And so came the day when Fran and I were seated at our usual table before Ramona and Fred arrived and were startled by this question, "Are these two seats taken?" Well, duh, we thought. Haven't you seen? Haven't they always been taken? But these were newcomers. They could not have known. And we knew the rule — no reserved seats. We had to reply, "No, these seats are not taken. Please join us." And two strange people whose faces have considerably been purged from memory sat in Ramona and Fred's seats. Moments later we watched in dismay as our chosen ones walked up, spotted the interlopers, and moved on as if they had been banished.

Not to be undone, our usual foursome began a deliberate conspiracy to break the no reserved seating rule. First, we all vowed to arrive early enough to grab all four seats before any usurper got there — often more easily plotted than done. Meals are important events; people arrive early. Then we moved to a different table down room to confuse the invaders. But we were quickly tracked down and forced apart again. A deliberate game of "Bust 'em up!" seemed underway, played by a group of both old and new residents and not without considerable glee. We played it out, gloating with glee each time we got the best of them.

In the process, we made another intriguing discovery. One day the servers began taking and delivering orders in the front of the room, just outside the kitchen. The next day they began from the rear. We realized that if we just made a daily move back and forth we could be forever first in line! It took but a couple of days for that ploy to become common knowledge and useless. The daily end-to-end shifting turned into a confusing scramble. Meanwhile, lots of people were laughing themselves silly. Not a bad thing.

Of course, managers Geena and Adam got wise to these shenanigans and put us all on notice. Assigned seats would never be imposed upon us. By the same token, reserved seats were not allowed. First come would be first seated anywhere they desired. And our dear managers knew that we would all be gracious enough to welcome any and all who might wish to join us at any table at any time. Wouldn't we? They also reminded us that Haven Lake residents are family. It should be our fervent desire to get to know, respect, enjoy and, yes, love one another. For that purpose there was no better melting pot than a dining room with open seating.

So one and all — well mostly all — behaved as instructed. And in the process all discovered that there were among our fellow residents a great number of interesting, likeable, enjoyable people. Three or four tables continue to be private domains — usually either all men or all women. But everyone has come to accept the idea that some personal preferences should be respected. Short of deliberate segregation, unthinkable in any case, dining room rules need not be slavishly followed — a conclusion we residents like to assert to our managers as often as necessary.

Without a doubt the dining room is an immensely effective melting pot. It is here that first acquaintances are made and weighed and sorted. Sorted for compatible personalities. Sorted for shared interests. Sorted for ways and means to find and activate and extend friendships that transcend the simple culinary experience. In the dining room we get to know who we are.

8.

Who *are* these old people?

The simple truth is this: The residents of Haven Lake are what we are, just as we see one another, just as we experience one another day after day in the here and now. Surprisingly, there is little curiosity and therefore minimum discussion about former occupations, events or experiences from our earlier years. Yes, everybody knows that I am an author; I put copies of my three previous books in the library. But Fran and I are better known as the couple who play a pretty good game of bridge right here and now.

Sure, we ask the new resident, "Where are you from?" Maybe we pursue that with, "And what did you do?" But these questions are more courteous than inquisitive. What we really want to know is how well can we get along with this individual as we live out each day together in Haven Lake.

There are about 70 people in residence in Haven Lake as this is written. There will be as many as 140 eventually. The last time most of us encountered such communal living was most likely in college and/or the military. Our biggest interpersonal relationship challenges were probably experienced in our careers. But we were young then. We were resilient. We could handle the abrasions, the give and take of forced togetherness and competitiveness. If we remember how we managed the stress and strife of those earlier days, if we are honest, we might admit that it was easy compared to the exigencies of our present community life.

"Community life." There's the rub! We are living in an environment, under a set of circumstances probably never before known to any of us. Most of us at Haven Lake are now over eighty! Set in our ways. Some might even say crotchety. Fussy for sure. We like to think we have learned patience over the years. But let someone or something upset our time-honored routines and hackles rise. The wonder is that we manage to get along as well as we do. But then we are octogenarians, a super breed. We are able to leap the tall buildings of vicissitude, to move like a speeding train along the paths of mutual love and respect. We are truly super people. Come meet some of us and see if you agree.

For starters, please remember beautiful, brave Brenda so dependant on her walker. And magnificent Winston with his kettle drum voice. Ramona and Fred are, as you know, at the top of our personal list of super people.

George and Judy, 90 and 83 respectively are as active and lively as a couple of teenagers. George and I shoot pool twice a week. Ask Judy about a game of cards and she'll offer a choice of twenty-five or more, ready to play anytime, anywhere.

Catherine (call her Hepburn) and Josh (call him Ichabod) are proof positive of the payoff for table hopping. We watched them time and again come and go from the dining room getting only the impression that Catherine was probably very shy and Josh not very talkative. Then we shared a table with them – and WOW! Put a question to Catherine and her face lights up with an eagerness to respond. Raise a topic with Josh and be prepared for enlightened discussion. What delightful, interesting, enjoyable people.

Queen Anne strides out of her nearby apartment, head held high, scans the dining room as if searching for those upon whom she will bestow her royal company — then sits as always at the same up front table. Prince consort Dan, tall, straight backed, still limping slightly from a recent hip replacement, joins her shortly. Lucky are those who gain the other seats at their table. Anne's throaty voice and twinkling eyes enhance all conversations. Lively discussions move freely and easily with constant stimuli from Dan.

Lynda and Gloria could be twin sisters. Constant companions to one another, side by side they are as lovely as a corsage of white carnations. Lynda moved here from our old neighborhood months before we did and encouraged us to follow. Gloria and my Fran first met in the corridor to the dining room where brief introductions led to instant compatibility and friendship. Wherever they sit, waves, smiles and blown kisses across the room keep these two close to us.

Big Paul, hale, hearty, 90 years young, was Haven Lake's first resident. He was born and raised within a quarter mile of the community and is now, of course, our historian.

Danyelle was blown our way by New Orleans's Katrina — husband, house, dog all lost in the great storm. Botched rescue efforts, inadequate health care, a series of stays in half-way houses did not break her happy spirit nor spoil her sweet smile. Just beware when you meet her at the poker table.

Nurse Janice (call her saint) spreads her loving concern and care far and wide to all who may or may not need it. First aid to Janice, trained in the military, means give help NOW, ask questions later. It is virtually impossible to keep track of her in the dining room. Her constant table hopping reveals a determination to get to know everyone before anyone might need her help.

Gary, the country music fiddler and former member of the Marine Special Forces. Talent and personality make Gary one of our most interesting and entertaining residents. When he launches an impromptu performance before the fireplace, all gather around to stomp and sing along.

Ada's outgoing charm permeated the room the first day she sat down to eat. The personification of black is beautiful, she quickly became a very active member of the community, just as we expected she would. A good game of competitive bridge is one of her greatest delights.

Tina, sweet, smiling, silent. A former star of women's semi-professional baseball. Forever seeking ways to be of service to others.

Nicholas and Jacalyn are the spice in the residential pot-pourri. Their tales of entrepreneurial enterprises, from antique shops to vintage auto shows fascinate us. Nicholas ties the author for the title of Chief Resident Gad Fly.

Youthful Paul and Marylou seem totally out of place, yet dominate the scene by their presence and participation in virtually every activity, every day. I made so bold as to approach them at dinner one day to ask point blank, "You are both obviously still in your early seventies, healthy, vibrant, active. Whatever are you doing here?" I was informed that they found this life akin to a perpetual ocean cruise — fun people, great food, perpetual entertainment, housekeeping service, no taxes to pay, no repairs to make. How could life get any better? Furthermore, they had tried out several retirement communities and deemed Haven Lake the best.

So, does this partial review of the resident roster mark us as one great, happy mutual admiration society? Let the answer to that come from someone else.

A beloved former pastor, Father Jim Hawker and I spent many grand times discussing organized religions and, especially, the people who profess them. One fine day he put his feelings on the line. "John," he said, "here's the truth. I love all my parishioners. I just like some of them a lot more than some others." Amen to that.

We shall waste no words disparaging any resident of Haven Lake. One man's mitzapuny soup is another man's chicken noodle. But one observation does need to be made. Any resident who might be disliked probably falls within one specific category — those who are impatient with or critical of the shortcomings and failures of others. As we here seek to demonstrate, only the elderly know what it is like to be elderly. Failure to sympathize with and support one another is an egregious fault not easily excused.

Otherwise, as has been noted, the elderly retain all the personal and social faults of our youth, we just manage them better. The futility of social conflict is better recognized. Our tolerance of one another is normally greater. Energy is reserved for the tasks of simple survival. For the most part we can all get along together — and do so remarkably well.

9.
"Thy Rod and Thy Staff."

If this chapter heading seems a bit sacrilegious, you need to know(1) that our subject is the Haven Lake staff, (2) that Geena heads it up, and (3) that The Holy Bible is, very simply, her guide book. She makes no apology for preaching the word of God at any and every opportunity. She will approve the following offering of chapter and verse as her introduction:

"The Lord is my shepherd, I shall not want; He leads me in paths of righteousness for His name's sake. Even though I walk through the valley of the shadow of death, I fear no evil, for Thou art with me; Thy rod and thy staff, they comfort me. Thou preparest a table before me in the presence of my enemies; Thou annointest my head with oil, my cup overflows. Surely goodness and mercy shall follow me all the days of my life; and I shall dwell in the house of the Lord forever." (Psalm 23:1-6 RSV)

Geena is the lay lord of Haven Lake.

Once a month or so a meeting of management and residents is held. Geena normally presides and must surely have Psalm 23 in mind as she repeatedly preaches about her total dedication to the well-being and happiness of each resident and the community as a whole. As the Lord cares for His flock, so Geena cares for her residents. Whenever she appears among us, her first cry is, "I love you!" And in case you don't hear her, she usually seals the message with hugs and noisy kisses for one and all.

Too precious? Just try her out for sincerity. At every management/resident meeting, she demands that we tell her about every grievance, however slight. Then she tells us that it *will* be fixed — or it will not be fixed if that is impossible, impractical or unwise in her judgment. Does she keep her promises? No one is keeping a record, but ask most residents and the response is sure to be, "Yes!"

Of course, Geena has help. Her husband Adam will welcome that revelation. His dedication to our well-being is second to hers only in the voicing, never in the doing. Two other husband and wife teams are assistant managers. Tyler and Caralee came on duty shortly before Haven Lake opened in late 2008. Matthew and Amelia were employed in July, 2009. As Geena proudly pointed out in her introductions of these people, all are deeply religious. They are a reflection of her belief that just as God is love so is love the business of Haven Lake.

All three couples live in the community as our next door neighbors. They have developed a work schedule (which we residents have never figured out) that enables them to get the managing job done without an impossible physical strain on any one of them. At all times, one or another couple is "on duty" to deal with any emergency that might strike either the facility or the residents. Every apartment is equipped with emergency pulls that can be used to call for management help — day or night. The alarms are sounded in the managers' apartments as well as in the main office day or night.

Additional staff people are Executive Chef Jacob, Sous Chef Carlos, Assistant Chef Mark, Enrichment Coordinator Ronny, Community Sales Representative Cameron, and Maintenance Manager Albert. These people are ever evident and active in community life. You have already heard and will hear much more about Chef Jacob. Ronny is like a perpetual motion machine setting up various activities and rounding up participants. Cameron pitches in wherever needed, but is at his best welcoming the many visitors groups — potential residents — he has lined up to dine and tour the premises and learn about Haven Lake. Albert is the quintessential jack of all trades. Virtually nothing mechanical that needs doing or fixing is beyond his capability.

Most of the work of the three managing couples is done behind the scenes in the office. But they also engage in a great deal of direct association with the residents and participate in many activities. They eat the very same food we do at nearby tables. It is a wonder they do not suffer perpetual indigestion because they eat and serve concurrently. Any one of them will at any time drop a fork or spoon after a bite, jump up from their table and rush to meet some resident need or request elsewhere in the dining room. Between courses, they roam the dining room, carafes in hand, refilling coffee and tea cups.

They also listen while they eat! We have discovered that if we sit as close as one or two tables from the managers' table they can

— and do — listen to our conversations. They make no bones about this. It is simply their desire to know our feelings about the food, certainly, but also any other subject with which they can deal. When first made aware of this, I tried to speak sotto voce. That quickly got tiresome and didn't work. A whispered complaint to a fellow diner about some dissatisfactory food serving got an instant response from Geena or Adam. One or the other was immediately at my side to ask if I'd like a replacement. This was so inevitable that it actually became a bit disconcerting. I began to stifle my complaints. But then I suspected that could be their intent. I was unwilling to give them that satisfaction. So we both now have it our own way. I continue to complain; they continue to listen and commiserate and correct.

While they always aim to please, the managers sometimes shoot at the wrong targets. Tyler, for example, decided that we should be amused. He bought a joke book and every evening before supper read a selection from it. How many things are wrong with that? The jokes were awful. The laughter they provoked was embarrassed and forced. Tyler was unhappy with this response. We felt patronized, misunderstood and demeaned. The jokes stopped. Tyler was credited with the wisdom to sense his error. But a few weeks later, he announced that the jokes would begin again. They had stopped, he explained, only because his wife, Caralee, had hidden the joke book. I shouted out, "Three cheers for Caralee!" The cheers rang out across the dining room and there have been no more jokes to amuse us.

Some time after Tyler's joke debacle Ronny decided that we should be mentally challenged with riddles. Every morning before breakfast she posed a silly riddle gleaned from some unannounced source. We were given until midday dinner to find the solution. All who came up with the correct solution were rewarded with "FUNNY MONEY." (Much more about FUNNY MONEY later.) How many things are wrong with that? I will not insult my readers with answers they already know. Ronny is a dear one, deeply dedicated to her task. I vowed to advise her to get rid of the riddles, but had no need. It took her but three or four riddles to discern that they were ill-advised and we have been challenged no more. Way to go, Ronny!

The first chapter of this book suggested that the managers of retirement communities may be devoted to us, but even they do not know what it is like to grow old. Geena might again approve a quotation from Scripture: "Forgive them, Father, for they know not what they do." But that would be an unwarranted prayer for their simple sin — killing with kindness.

"Killing with kindness" begs for examples. Read about response to accidents in the next chapter. Many more might be offered, but to no real purpose. The managers love us. That is the simple fact. They strive mightily to achieve our total happiness. If they fail in some ways it is because they attempt the impossible. Until they are in their eighties, like us, they will never totally know how to make us totally happy — as if that were ever possible. Let it simply be known that we love them dearly for trying and none the less if they sometimes fail.

Before we leave the managers, let's enjoy some scuttlebutt, a divergence in which we elderly in community have been known to indulge.

When Matthew and Amelia were hired as a third managing couple, many of us wondered why. Was a community less than two-thirds occupied that hard to manage? Were the residents that obstreperous? Were Tyler and Caralee in trouble? There was cause to consider the latter possibility.

Tyler is a hands-on, no-nonsense manager. He plays by the rules as he interprets them. If he disagrees with us, we know it. If he believes something is good — or bad — for us, we know it. With supreme self-confidence, he has made known his desire and expectation to one day become head manager of a community and eventually ascend to a corporate management position. Commendable, you say. Yes, until this question looms large: Who is really in charge of Haven Lake?

At a manager/resident meeting, Geena felt the need to answer this question. She stated her very high regard for the Tyler-Caralee team, but reminded us that they are assistant managers, not head managers. She respects Tyler's ambitions and will support them when and if she believes he is ready for top management responsibilities. In the meantime, Geena and Adam run Haven Lake. 'Nuff said!

But not enough done. Shortly thereafter, Tyler and Caralee vanished for a week, reportedly on a training assignment at another facility. Next, they took a week's vacation in Florida. As this is written, they have been absent for over two weeks, again reportedly on a training mission.

Speculation about the purpose and possible culmination of these shenanigans slithers through the community. Two things are obvious: (1) Haven Lake can be managed very well, thank you, by just two management couples. (2) Matthew and Amelia have been welcomed and are very well liked by the residents. No odious comparisons have been made, at least not openly, but the big money is betting that Tyler and Caralee will not again be permanent managers at Haven Lake.

With some justification, readers may well ask, "What has any of this management stuff got to do with the kind of life residents experience or desire? Aren't all of you just too nosy and catty for your own good?" Goodness gracious, the Tyler and Caralee saga is high drama, great entertainment, shades of enthralling events from our own past lives. Ronny at her best could not devise a greater diversion from our aches and pains and worries. But most significantly, this titillating tale highlights the significance of the managers in our daily lives. They can and do make a difference for better or for worse.

BULLETIN: Speculation has just become fact. Caralee has returned to Haven Lake. Tyler has not. Next Monday Caralee will supervise movers who will relocate them to a community in New Hampshire where they will again resume the duties of assistant managers. Caralee is enthusiastic. "They don't even have horse racing up there," she exclaims. "And no FUNNY MONEY. Tyler is really shaking them up." Some elderly people in New Hampshire will soon learn the significance of management people in their lives.

10.
These feet were meant for walking!

But that's not what they do! (If this take-off on long ago famous lyrics grabs you, you are surely one of us.)

If present trends continue, and mankind does not annihilate itself in the meantime, 1000 years from now people will live to be 150. If Darwin was correct, 10,000 years from now people over 80 will gradually revert from two-legged to four-legged mobility. Nature will have recognized and corrected the simple fact that after 80 years two legs are just no damn good!

Some evolutionists posit that four-legged mobility will actually occur at birth. We elderly do not support that view. Only when you lose it can you appreciate how much fun two legs have provided. One example will suffice: Is there anything more glorious than a man and women enfolded in one another's arms.

Try that on four legs! Nature is smart enough to keep what's good while correcting what's bad.

Enough! As my grandson John would say, "'Snot funny, grampa!"

People over eighty suffer many ailments. Many are internal and not obvious to others — except for an oxygen tank or two — unless we talk or complain about them, which most in Haven Lake do not do. But mobility problems are right out there for all to see.

At meal times, walkers of various designs and functions line the outer walls of the dining room like taxis awaiting fares at the airport. Some are simple four-footed devices made of aluminum piping with wheels on two feet and plastic skids on the other two feet. These are simply lifted step by step or pushed along by handles. The skids provide enough traction to keep the devices from flipping out from under and dropping the user to the ground. Others are fancy four-wheeled devices constructed of brightly painted tubular steel, fitted with storage baskets, seats and hand brakes. House rules stipulate that all such walkers must be kept out of the actual dining area lest they become hazardous obstructions to diners and servers.

This stricture creates another problem not dealt with in the rules. How do those who use the walkers — because they really need them — travel from parking spot to table? The answer is simple and sweet. Other residents leap to their assistance with whatever hand or arm holding is necessary to help them cover these final few feet. Or they get them seated and then remove the walker to a parking spot.

Walking canes are a simpler means to steadier, safer mobility. Though few are in use, they also pose a storage problem. Hooked on the back or arm of a chair they become very possible tripping devices for the servers. Laid flat on the floor beside the chair is little better. Laid across a seat says, "This seat is taken." Not allowed. Yet for some reason, the very sensible idea of parking them beside walkers along the side walls has simply not taken hold and has not been mandated. Two possible reasons come to mind. (1) The walking cane is a much more intimate possession than a walker and is not to be left much out of hand. (2) The two devices have distinctively different social significances.

Disturbing thought, perhaps. But think! How many movies or TV shows have you seen in which walking — or dancing — canes have been starred? Remember Fred Astaire? Jimmy Cagney? Now think again. How many walkers have you seen so exalted? There are no canes in Haven Lake comparable to the showpiece my grandfather flaunted in his latter years with its ebony shaft, silver fittings and ivory carved head. But it is a simple fact: Canes are as socially significant as they are useful. Walkers are just a necessity.

The ultimate aid to mobility is the wheelchair. There are three or four in Haven Lake that are propelled by hand or foot. At least one more is a fancy motorized model. All are privileged. Not because of Raymond Burr's TV portrayal of handicapped Chief Detective Robert T. Ironside, but out of necessity. Owners must and are allowed to drive them right up to the table. Servers or other residents will readily remove the usual table chair to make room for them.

This book is not a medical manual. But in addition to the devices that improve elderly mobility we do need to talk about the physical problems that force their use. For that, we will use a case in point — my own.

The first symptoms were felt probably in my early eighties. I reported to my doctor that I was losing equilibrium. "When I walk the dog, I feel like I'm listing to the right." He had me walk a few steps with my eyes closed and proclaimed that I was remarkably stable for my years but should expect the sensation to persist and probably increase over time. For some time I experienced no reason for further concern. Then one day three or so years ago, Maggie, our beautiful beagle, pulled me off my feet as we were walking on uneven grass. That terrain got both blame for the fall and thanks that I was not injured. But this incident was the beginning of serious worry about the possibilities and dangers of falling.

Medical media warn repeatedly about the dangers of poor mobility and the damage that can result from falls, but I was totally unprepared for what I saw and experienced upon arrival at Haven Lake. In addition to those residents who use canes, walkers and wheel chairs, a majority of the rest of us show clear evidence of some degree of impaired mobility. We shuffle and stagger and sway. We teeter and totter and toddle. And we tumble and fall — as I did once again. And then yet again!

Maggie was also involved in both additional falls. The two of us, man and dog, get healthy exercise from three or four daily circumnavigations of the community, one-quarter mile each time around. My cardiologist considers Maggie my best medicine. Not so on the day she suddenly zigged at the end of her leash just as I zagged. Balance lost, I dropped to the pavement hard on my right hip and elbow. Luck was with me that day. Nothing was broken. Ice packs soon reduced a grapefruit-sized lump on the hip. Copious bandaging applied by Fran stopped the bleeding of the elbow. And a deep purple bruise about six inches wide by two feet long on my hip gradually disappeared in three to four weeks.

It was a warning I vowed to heed. Maggie has always been a good follower for a beagle, and I began to hold her leash with only one finger. If she wanted to take off she could — without me! I knew she would never stray far.

The circumstances of my next fall were much different and more drastic. Maggie and I were on our usual walk when another small dog came out of nowhere, unleashed and snapping at Maggie. As quickly as I can tell it, Maggie's leash, loose hold not withstanding, was wrapped around my legs and down I went. The full weight of my body landed on my left arm on the hood of a parked Cadillac. I fell from there to the pavement where my forehead hit and slid, peeling off a layer of skin.

While I cussed her out, the dog's owner kept crying, "I'm sorry, I'm sorry." But what is important for purposes of our discussion about the pros and cons of life in a retirement community is that help arrived immediately with Co-manager Matthew instantly on the scene. How he knew what had happened I never did find out. With his help I picked myself up, cradled an obviously broken left arm in my right hand, ignored the blood running into my eyes, and headed for my apartment. Maggie, good dog, followed me just as I knew she would.

By the time I reached our apartment a minute or two later, Geena was there! She washed and dressed my head and arm, fashioned a temporary splint from a book and had me fully prepped when daughter Ginny shortly arrived to drive me to the ER. At the ER, x-rays confirmed a broken left arm just above the wrist. An MRI ruled out any internal head damage. The arm was fitted with a splint and sling, which I was told I would be sporting for at least six to eight weeks.

Our neighbor, Nurse Janice, volunteered to walk Maggie for the next three weeks while I was unable to do so. That's when I began calling her Saint Janice.

What is important here is that my two falls were not singular events in Haven Lake. Beautiful Brenda tells of her repeated falls and fractures. Little Carla just recently removed a cast and sling from her shoulder. Yet, with a wry sense of the purposeful, I view my own fracture as providential. (Thank you, Lord!) It has supplied first-hand, timely fodder for these tales of elderly mobility. It has made the fear of falling that afflicts the elderly very much mine to know and to share with my readers. It has made the importance of a caring community such as Haven Lake a personal experience to extol and share with my readers.

And so it is. We waddle, we wobble, we wiggle! And we go whump! But we are a sanguine lot. We know how to strike a balance between the good stuff and the bad stuff. Life is a kaleidoscope of experiences for the beleaguered elderly. Let's take a further look into that multi-faceted, colorful display.

11.
Give me some room!

"It is really all I need, just for myself." When you hear these words, you know they have been spoken by a widow living in a studio apartment. The statement is undoubtedly true, but usually redolent of wistful recollections of much more spacious habitats of the past.

The studio apartments in Haven Lake are simply one L-shaped room. The door from the building main hall leads past a sink, small cabinet and refrigerator that constitute a "kitchen" into the sitting room area. These form one leg of the L shaped unit. The second leg of the L is the sleeping area. There is no physical separation between the two legs. A door from the sleeping area opens onto a small patio on the first floor and onto a balcony on the second and third floor apartments. When Janice invited me one day to a visit her first floor apartment through this outside door, I was shocked to find myself standing right next to her bed.

Almost apologetic, she said, "Yes, it is small, but it's really all I need."

The greatest blessing of these units may be their affordability. They offer space for TV viewing, reading, sleeping and not much more. Janice's apartment has a small plastic folding table tucked into the inner corner of the L that she uses for correspondence. Occupants of these studio apartments rely almost entirely upon community sponsored activities to fill their days, their lives. Yet every one I know is quite happy to have it that way.

A step up is the one bedroom apartment. Here, at least, living and sleeping quarters are physically separated. Each area also has a bit more square footage for better furnishings and perhaps more varied usages. George and Judy invited me into their third floor apartment one day and proudly showed me the beautiful view of the lake from their balcony and the unique triangular computer console built by their talented son into the corner of the bedroom.

"I suppose we could use another bedroom," Judy opined, "but this is really all we need."

"It's all you wanted to pay for," George reminded her.

"Well, that's because it is all we need," she repeated.

If Judy is correct, then the largest apartments, with two bedrooms and two baths, could be providing much more space than any one person or couple might really need. Certainly they cost much more to rent than most residents can or are willing to afford. As a consequence, no doubt, there are only twelve of them available — two at both ends of the building on each of three floors. Of course, all contain more square footage in all rooms than any other units. This provides space for many more furnishings, if nothing else, if that is one's desire.

Indeed, most of our living room furnishings were moved to Haven Lake and fit exceptionally well — much to the delight of our daughters. Ginny observes, "Mom and Dad, in your past two homes you spent most of your waking hours in either a den or a sunroom. The living rooms were never used except for company and big family gatherings. Now you are finally living in a living room!" And, in fact, we very much like it that way. Large windows on two walls make it sunny, if not a "sun" room, and give us a spectacular view of woods and lake.

But the second bedroom and bath in these units make the biggest difference. There are many options for the use of that extra space, although I know of none that is used as a guest bedroom. The community reserves one suite that may be rented for that purpose if need be. Our own second bedroom has multiple uses. A large fully filled bookcase and cluttered desk occupy one entire wall. The opposite wall accommodates my computer console beneath a solid wall display of family photos and paintings next to a sizeable closet. My electronic keyboard nestles beneath the large window on a third wall. The closet and bath with shower have been designated for my personal use.

All of this is fine with Fran. The master bath and two closets are hers alone. So is most of the large closet that stretches the length of the entrance hall. With much help in the gleaning process from our daughters, she gave a large quantity of clothing to the Salvation Army before we moved, but still retains a more than adequate and varied selection for any possible need in our new home and lifestyle.

But if the two bedroom set-up sounds pretty grand, consider this catch 22. The more one finds to do in the apartment, the less appeal one finds in community activities. And it doesn't do to say that two bed-roomers have the best of both worlds. Many days there is the feeling that you have the lesser of both worlds. Many of the amenities a full house used to provide are truly gone. Yet the extra space of two bedrooms simply makes it more difficult to adapt to a 100% community lifestyle.

Such crazy anomalies would not normally come to mind before the decision is made to move to a retirement community. Yet they could have a significant bearing on that decision as well as the choice of apartment size. That's pretty important. And now you have heard about it here.

One of the axioms for how to manage the aging process is to simplify, simplify, simplify. Another is to economize, economize, economize. Who is to say that those who chose a studio apartment were not the smarter ones?

12.
I hear you knocking, but you can't come in!

"I hear you knocking ..." was first voiced to me by a fellow seminarian some 70 years ago. Yes, a seminarian.

"I know what you mean," she said, "but the grass is wet" was an expression of comparable meaning often heard from a fellow ad man some 45 years ago.

One or the other, both expressions announce that our subject, at last, has got to be sex among the senior set.

Aha! Been waiting for this one, haven't we? Let's just hope that you are not disappointed, because here comes an example of the kind of salacious stuff you are about to hear.

Fran and I are often seen walking down the long corridor from our apartment to the Haven Lake dining room holding hands. This display of affection elicits observations along these lines: "Isn't that sweet? They've been married 65 years and still hold hands." But they should know what readers have learned from a previous chapter. We are actually just trying to prevent one another from falling.

In preparation for this chapter on senior sex, I've had to make some coy inquiries because, truth to tell, there is little overt evidence of any kind of hanky-panky among our fellow residents.

"See any romances budding," I've been forced to ask.

"Nope," is the scintillating response usually received.

For some time, the only promising clue to an actual affair was an all too audible whisper James made to Joyce one evening as she passed behind his dining room chair, "Three knocks on the door. Okay?" This provoked such ribald laughter at the time that there has been no sign of anything between the two since then. No one knows whether a budding romance was in the works or was unkindly shattered at the get-go.

Other snippets of conversation picked up at mealtime (Paul is putting drops in Danyelle's eyes) suggest that a couple of amorous pursuits and even competitions are most probably if not in fact underway. But to outward appearances, we are just a bunch of men and women enjoying one another's company and companionship and behaving quite properly.

Statistically, at this writing there are 12 married couples, 18 single men and 57 single women residing in Haven Lake. That would seem to stock the odds for romance very much against the single women. This ratio of a bit more than three-to-one single women over single men exceeds U.S. Census data for 2008 in which men make up 1.2% and women 2.05% of the total over 80 population. The opportunities for women to find romance in

Haven Lake are not quite as good as they are in the nation as a whole.

Thus, if my math is viable and sybaritic action is truly minimal in Haven Lake, it may be due to this unbalanced availability of possible partnerships.

On the other hand, we may simply be faced with these questions: Do any of the singles, men or women, give a damn about romance? Is the thought of sex after 80 futile? Is it just uninteresting? Might it be offensive to some people? Or is some very real action taking place that I am just missing?

Hoping for some kind of answers to such questions, I decided to speak to a voice of experience — Geena.

Oh my, Geena has no doubt that sex can and does remain very much alive in the thoughts and actions of the elderly — or some of them, for sure. She gave me a couple of tales from former communities in which she has served to make her point and to share with you.

Two daughters of a gentleman resident appeared in her office one day in tears. When she asked the reason for their distress, they cried, "It's daddy!"

"What about daddy?" Geena was forced to ask.

"We found bobby pins in his bed!" they wailed.

"And so?" Geena asked.

"He's having an affair with some woman!"

"And so?" Geena asked again. She knew all about the couple and their frequent liaisons. They were consenting adults. She assured the daughters there was no need for their distress. Indeed, she informed me, the couple, well into their 80's, eventually left the community, got married and purchased a private home in Arizona where they lived happily together for many more years.

Another time there was the gentleman who had an electronic organ in his third floor apartment upon which he was wont to play romantic music into the wee hours of the night. Then he would stroll down the corridor knocking on the doors of single ladies asking if they would like a massage. Geena never learned how many massages, if any, were given. But the complaints of harassment she received were numerous. She summoned the culprit to her office and ordered him to cease and desist from his massaging enterprise. To assure compliance she moved him to a first floor apartment across the corridor from her own. And she advised him that if he did not put an end to his shenanigans, he and his organ would be removed from the community — and not just the one with a keyboard!

We are indebted to Geena for these revealing tales. They represent perhaps the best and the worst examples of interpersonal relationships that might be assayed in a community of the elderly. But the truth is more likely this:

Feelings of love and sex are probably much the same among the elderly as they are within the population as a whole. Sexual attraction between men and women is in the head and knows no age. Sexual performance is a bodily function that might or might not be affected by age — or by pills, for that matter. Beyond this, what happens behind closed doors is nobody's business, say we at Haven Lake.

NEWS FLASH! Janice and Ryan are engaged. Yes, the very same "Saint" Janice. But you don't yet know Ryan. He is tall, surely six feet, has a full head of thick, wavy, salt and pepper hair, is ruggedly handsome and soft spoken. Truly a personification of the gracious southern gentleman. In the eyes of all of us, it is a totally perfect pairing.

Yet we are as much surprised as pleased. It has been but a few weeks since we first became aware of their interest in one another. And Janice says the wedding will take place in less than a month. We shake our heads and then screw them on straight again and say, "Well, why on earth should it not be fast?" Time for all of us is of the essence. The approval of others is of no consequence. The lengthy, tedious planning that normally precedes a youthful, first marriage has no relevance here. They are in love. They will marry. That is how it should be. We wish them great happiness.

Let all widows and widowers who are contemplating a move to a retirement community give careful heed to this lovely romance. Everyone knows without question, of course, that finding a new mate has not been the motive for anyone's move to a retirement community. Gracious, no! Memories of a lost loved one remain fresh and sorrowful. Replacement is unthinkable. Yet we have now heard here of two marriages with which residents of retirement communities have been blessed.

As this book was in final editing, Janice and Ryan were married. And a second Haven Lake couple whom readers have not met exchanged their vows before the fireplace in the dining room in a beautiful ceremony arranged by Geena. Both couples held their receptions in our Activity Room.

The odds for meaningful romances may be better than the population figures portend. It would seem prudent, at the very least, to keep an open mind.

And make no mistake: Two can most definitely live cheaper than one in a retirement community if that should matter.

Whatever the realities in respect to romance, there is a tendency of the young to characterize the elderly as some form of nobility — staid, steady, serious, well beyond the sexual foibles of common people. Our children, especially, like to think of us this way. They cannot envision us behaving any other way.

They are not alone in their concern. Some younger people with whom I have discussed this book admonish me to keep my elder contemporaries on a pedestal of high respectability. One gets the impression that they do not want to be forced to defend their own reputations when they, too, get to be 80.

In actual fact, we do not easily fit into any exalted role created for us. We do not aspire to any form of sanctity that is not related to some idea of an afterlife. We simply try to live and enjoy quite normal lives, which is difficult enough.

Read on!

13.
"Out, damn'd spot!"

Among the issues that consume the national psyche in the beginning years of the second millennium, physical abuse is near the top of the list. Investigators of this aberration go bonkers when they behold the elderly. Put 50 random Haven Lake residents in a police line-up, order them to bare their arms and legs, and you will see 50 suspected cases of physical abuse. What alarms investigators are bruises. Multiple bruises. Big bruises. Little bruises. Purple bruises. Pink bruises. If we are not getting beaten, they wonder, where do all these bruises come from?

We visit the doctor and the prep nurse asks, "Do you have any problems with personal relationships?' She wants to ask, "Who has been beating you?" Doctors, of all people, should understand this phenomenon — they are largely responsible for it. Strokes are a major threat for the elderly. Blood thinners are the most commonly prescribed stroke preventatives. Almost everyone these days, young or old, takes some aspirin dose daily in order to benefit from any one or more of the "miracles" it is purported to perform. Add doses of other blood thinners like Coumadin or Plavix, all too well known to the elderly, all frequently prescribed by our doctors, and your blood becomes a witch's brew for bruises. Factor in the thinning of the epidermis, that cushioning between our blood vessels and the brutal outside world that is naturally experienced by the elderly, and what have you got? Thin blood. Thin skin. The slightest bump. Big bruise!

Fortunately, our damned spots do not have the significance of Lady Macbeth's bloody damned spots. But they are part of the mosaic that paints who and what we are. We make the same tired jokes about them again and again. Who smacked you this time? What do you mean you don't know how you got it? Are you losing it? Tell the old coot he's squeezing you too tight. We laugh them off.

Then some callous young person feels compelled to tell us how horrible these bloody bruises make us look and we are suddenly transported back to a painful adolescence, reminded of the shame, the unfairness and the agony of zits. What goes around comes around, every bit as hurtful.

Yet all in all, we are really quite fond of our bruises. They are the one ailment among all that afflict the elderly that we can freely talk and laugh about because it is not the ailment that is going to kill us. Bruises are not cancer. They are not a stroke. They are not heart failure. They are not broken bones that refuse to heal. They are not stomach ulcers. They are not Alzheimer's disease. They are nothing to worry about in our whole world of medical worries.

There is an opening here to plunge into that whole world of elderly medical worries. It is without doubt a significant subject and not to be ignored. There are endless tales to be told, both heroic and heartbreaking. But we are going to take a pass on this for a number of reasons. The subject is incredibly complex with an almost never-ending lexicon of possible maladies. Any meaningful discussion would require an expertise I do not possess. The most compelling deterrent might be its morbidity. We who deal with health problems on a daily basis have no desire to discuss them at length. We get enough of that with our doctors, too often if not at sufficient length. I hope my readers agree that they do not want to read all about them here.

So, avoiding that morass, lovingly nursing our bruises, let us get back to the reality show that is our daily life at Haven Lake.

14.
What do these old people *do*?

We are over 80 years old. We find it difficult to stay on our feet. We often can't remember what it was we intended to do ten minutes ago. Or we can't remember how to do it. Clearly there must not be all that much that we are able to do. We sleep eight or nine hours each night (hopefully). We spend four to five hours eating three meals a day. We nap a couple of hours every afternoon. It seems as if we spend half our lives waiting in doctors' offices. Clearly we must not have all that much free time to do anything more.

"'Snot funny grampa!" Okay, grandson John, here's the serious side of things.

A large escutcheon mounted on the wall of the main staircase in Haven Lake displays this corporate motto:

Seniors serving seniors; seniors serving society.

And beneath that escutcheon, a large plaque admonishes residents:

Don't just live with us, participate with us.

Clearly, these posted communications tell us what corporate managers expect us to be doing. They are daunting challenges. We need to explore the meaning of each in the reality of our daily lives. We need to examine the extent to which they are achieved — or not.

"Seniors serving seniors; seniors serving society" is one of those noble sounding platitudes that cannot be faulted for either its good intent or promotional value. It attempts to put the lie to the easy, perhaps too prevalent perception of retirement community residents as a bunch of useless, doddering old fuddy-duddies. This former marketing man gives it a nod of approval from that perspective. Whether or not it is happening is another question.

To properly appraise this claim or expectation, if that is what it is, we must consider the two parts separately.

"Seniors serving seniors" does happen a lot. Several examples within the community have been cited earlier. There will be more. We are all in the same boat. Anyone in obvious need of any immediate or continuing help gets it, as often from a fellow resident as from a staff member, simply because we are on the spot.

"Seniors serving society" is something else again. This very broad idea of elderly service is not yet a stated goal for Haven Lake residents, either by us or by management. It is not even a topic for current discussion. This could change, of course, if we residents decide on our own to launch such an initiative. Or if Ronny, our Enrichment Coordinator, comes to see such an endeavor as her responsibility and initiates some action. Neither possibility seems imminent.

On the other hand, that emphatic charge, "Don't just live with us, participate with us," opens up a whole line of questioning about what retirement living should really be all about. The first time I read it (probably on a tour of the facility before we moved in) it was bothersome. Now that we have lived in Haven Lake for almost a year and better understand what it purports, I like it no better.

First of all, it issues a command. That is not likeable. We are residents of an *independent living* community, not members of the military. Second, it commands a form of action that we might not have foreseen when we chose this new life and might not now wish to pursue.

At a residents/managers meeting, I boldly expressed this possibility. We applaud every effort management makes to help us live meaningful, fulfilling, happy latter years, I stated. But we reject the idea that we must participate as management sees fit in such activities as management deems best for us! We especially reject the idea that anyone should be censored for any perceived failure to participate. Residents in attendance at that meeting gave this little speech a round of applause.

Of course we want activities, occupations, diversions to enhance our days, stimulate our minds and heal our bodies. And most all of us are active participants in a variety of "enrichment" programs initiated by Ronny. It is just the sense of being ordered — or bribed as we shall see later — that raises the hackles.

By the way, don't you just love Ronny's job description — Enrichment Coordinator? Whatever happened to Social Director? How much of our monthly rent pays the clever copywriter in corporate headquarters who thought up that sobriquet? Sounds like a good description for a developer of fast foods at Kraft!

"'Snot funny grampa." I know, John, but how can one resist?

In fact, Ronny is dedicated to our service and gets good support from headquarters. She recently distributed a "Resident Enrichment Program Questionnaire" designed to help us decide upon and inform her of specific activities and programs we would enjoy and support. It is a four page document that leaves virtually no possibility unexplored. Consider just these section headings, each of which offers as many as 20 to 30 responses and choices:

Personal History

Lifestyle Activities

Local Community Activities

Intellectual and Cultural Activities

Physical and Relaxation Activities

Social Activities

Seniors Serving Seniors

Seniors Serving Society.

Note the familiar two at the end of the list. How come they are last here when they are emblazoned on the walls? Are they in fact just words?

The fault with this questionnaire is its daunting length. More than one resident has told me, "I can't be bothered filling out all that stuff." To which Ronny would surely protest, "Then how can I help to initiate programs and activities you want and would enjoy?"

In reality, it comes down to these two questions: Are the activities and programs now in place meeting residents' needs and desires? Do we need or desire any more and, if so, what should they be?

All of the following are regularly scheduled current activities, many of them daily, others at least once a week:

Sunday School

Chapel

Horse Racing

Exercise Class

Bingo

Skip-Bo Card Game

Wii Bowling

Jeopardy

Billiards

Bridge Games

Poker

Crafty Crafters

Conversation Corner

Willow Walkers

Swap Recipes Hour

Drawing classes

Now let's ask again in turn our two questions.

First, are these activities meeting resident's needs and desires?

In the strictest sense of the word, none of them are needed. Maybe Sunday School and Chapel for spiritual enrichment. Maybe Exercise Class for good health. Maybe Conversation Corner for broadening our social and political inquisitiveness and knowledge. All the rest are fun and games. They get us together for friendly competition, for creative endeavors, for good times and for passing time. There is enthusiastic participation by varying numbers of residents in all of these activities.

Ample facilities are provided in which to pursue them. A large first floor activities room. On the second floor, a well-equipped exercise room, well stocked, library, card game and billiards rooms, TV viewing room, reading room,. A chapel is located on the third floor.

Second, with so much on our plates, do we need or desire any more activities and, if we did, what should they be?

Many of the activities on the current list were initiated by residents. Most of them are organized and conducted by residents, with no complaints from a busy management. If one of us gets an idea or a yen for something new, this do-it-yourself process will undoubtedly be repeated. But no one is raising any hue and holler for more to do. And if we refuse to fill out Ronny's questionnaire, we will never know what exciting additional possibilities could be in store for us.

What we've got is what we've got, like it or not. If we like an activity, we participate. If we dislike another activity, we don't participate. A few residents simply do not choose to participate in much of anything, which is most certainly their prerogative.

This simple process of pick and choose works well with the routine, day by day activities. But it comes apart when we turn our attention to another category of activities, Special Events! Now we wade into muddy waters!

Special Events are Ronny's private bailiwick. She searches for events she believes we will enjoy. She chooses from many that are offered to her by outsiders, some of whom have self-serving interests. She schedules them approximately once a week. In recent months we were invited to participate in the following:

AARP Driving Class

Magic Night

Marty Vanderlip Singing

Sing Along With Rachel

Shag Lessons

SPCA Dog Wash

Belltone Hearing Test

Mystery Trip

Sarah Evans Piano

Al Stone Singing

Estates and Wills

Free Spinal Screening

Speaker Pam Yelton

Motivational Speaker

Sock Hop

Clearly, this is an eclectic lot that is bound to generate varying levels of interest from the residents. Yet Ronny feels obligated to drum up good attendance for all of them. She needs to justify her selections. If a peddler has something to sell us, she hopes we will want to buy. If she pays a performance fee, she needs to justify that cost. If presenters are volunteers, she wants them to feel appreciated. She is not above cajoling us to attend. She reminds us of that questionable command, "Don't just live with us, participate with us."

Public announcements are the primary method employed to get us to participate. Over a building-wide broadcast system we first hear loud chimes, "bing, bong, bing bong," repeated three times. This gets our attention. A stentorian announcement of an imminent event follows, delivered by one or another member of the staff. These disturbances are heard several times a day. The chimes penetrate walls and doors and are clearly heard within our apartments — quite annoying in the middle of an afternoon nap. The spoken announcements usually cannot be heard within the apartment well enough to understand them. This means, of course, that only those residents wandering the halls or already occupied with some activity in a public room get the full "benefit" of this practice. Once in a while we will hear the chimes at an odd time and out of shear curiosity open our hall door to hear the announcement. Rarely does this inspire us to get up and go. Given the repetitive schedule of many events, one often hears the chimes at a given time and knows the announcement that will follow without hearing it.

All in all, one must wonder if the benefit of these announcements outweighs the aggravation they give us. No one has yet deemed them sufficiently annoying to launch a protest against their invasion of our peace and quiet, though some say it would be justified. Many do believe that Ronny has a better idea. She prints and slips under our doors every Monday morning a list of all the activities scheduled for the coming week. Maybe someday this quiet alternative will replace the noisome broadcast announcements.

Between the announcements, the corridors are filled with canned music non-ending from dawn to dusk. Some residents like it. Others do not. In either case, its main impact is to constantly remind us that we live in an institution and no longer in our own home.

With the variety of activities offered via such iffy communications, it is not surprising that an occasional special event lays an egg. And when that happens, we are likely to suffer management disapproval. "We went to great effort to obtain this speaker," we were told recently, "and were embarrassed by the poor attendance." Well, duh! Did you ask us ahead of time if we might enjoy this speaker? Did you effectively describe the event to everyone? Did you give us sufficient announcement and reminders of the event? Do we really have to attend just because you say so?

Ronny has at her disposal and aggressively employs another surprisingly effective incentive to get us off our duffs, out of our apartments and into action — FUNNY MONEY!

When cajoling us or commanding us fails, FUNNY MONEY may succeed. It is printed on the office computer in denominations of $50, $100, $500, $1,000, $3,000 and $5,000. A schedule of FUNNY MONEY payouts has been issued. Every time we participate in an activity or attend a special event we are awarded a specified FUNNY MONEY payment. Every time we win in a competitive event, we receive a specified FUNNY MONEY prize award. So far, Sunday School and Chapel are not on the list.

Management is not above using FUNNY MONEY as a bribe. As much as $5,000 has been offered for attendance at management/resident meetings, even though they are not included in the payout schedule.

Managing these many and massive payoffs is a daunting task. If it is not properly and fairly done, some residents are not above complaining. We want our FUNNY MONEY when due and in the correct amount due! It got beyond Ronny's ability to keep up. She delegated the task to a number of volunteers. That put everyone on the honor system. Self appointed payout monitors are now at work in all activities. Residents total their balances like modern day Midases. FUNNY MONEY rules Haven Lake as surely as the real green rules Wall Street!

"'Snot funny grampa!" I know, little John. I'm not trying to be funny. Just listen to what FUNNY MONEY is good for.

About every other month, management conducts a big auction in the Activities Room. An array of items of varied kind and value, purchased or gathered from who knows where, is displayed and put up for bidding. FUNNY MONEY is the medium. These auctions are among the most eagerly awaited, most heavily attended, most fun events of the calendar year.

STOP THE PRESSES FOR A SPECIAL BULLETIN:

First annual Haven Lake
Sock Hop a total flop!

The decorations in the central lobby and Activity Room were spectacular. Strings of miniature CD's were hung from the main chandelier and every light fixture and festooned around every doorway. A dance floor was set in place in the center of the Activity Room. Two DJ's set up an array of audio equipment in the front of the room and were ready to perform. Cameron was setting up a table of soft drinks and snacks in the lobby. Preparations for this very special Special Event were lavish and complete. Your reporter was there at the 2:00 PM scheduled start time. Tina was there also, looking confused. She attends everything. But she and I made up a total attendance of two! Co-manager Matthew stood at the Activity Room entrance looking stunned. I asked him, "Who ever supposed that a sock hop would appeal to the residents of Haven Lake?"

"I don't know," he replied. "Not my job."

It is Ronny's job, of course. She arranged it all, but she is not here. I'm told she is at home nursing an injured back. All in all, we have a disaster in the making.

"Keep it funny, grampa," I now hear grown grandson John admonish.

Suppose I just tell the truth and let you decide whether to laugh or cry. We must go back a few days to set the stage.

On Tuesday of this week, Manager Adam announced at noon dinner that Haven Lake would sponsor a celebrity car in the huge Labor Day "Matthew's Alive" festival parade to be held the coming weekend. We will vote for resident King and Queen to ride in that vehicle. Nominations can be made until Thursday. Voting will take place at Friday dinner. The winners will be announced at the First Annual Sock Hop Friday afternoon.

Ballots were distributed Friday noon for immediate voting. Co-manager Amelia advised that the winners would be announced at the Sock Hop at 3:00 PM that afternoon! Not the 2:00 PM starting time. She later acknowledged that this 3:00 PM announcement time was a ploy intended, hopefully, to keep the Sock Hop alive for at least an hour.

At 2:00 PM I said to Tina, "I don't think anyone else will be here until three o'clock when we will hear who were voted King and Queen." At 2:15 we were still alone. The DJ was unhappily playing to an empty house. I said to Tina, "Let's leave and come back about three." And so we did.

At 2:50, as expected, there were 25 to 30 people seated along the walls of the Activity Room. Rock music blared away. No one was dancing. 3:00 PM came and went. A few more people showed up. Ada took to the dance floor. "Let's get this party rolling," she cried shuffling a few steps to the persistent loud music. Judy joined her briefly. Both soon gave up and retired to their seats. The DJ gave it a try, offering to dance with anyone who would volunteer to join him. No takers. Some feet were tapping among the seated residents in remembered recognition of long ago syncopations. Some surely would have danced if their ancient bodies could have danced. Most sat and stared with stunned disbelief at the extent of the unfolding fiasco.

At 3:20 PM I said to Matthew, "Can somebody please announce the winners of King and Queen and take these people out of their misery?" He scurried off. A few minutes later co-manager Amelia skittered into the room totally out of breath. (We later learned that she had been conducting a tour for potential residents, which Matthew had interrupted.) She set up two chairs in the middle of the dance floor and finally announced the winners of the King and Queen election. Fancy robes were draped over Big Paul and Nurse Janice. King Paul got his scepter. Queen Janice got here crown.

These two very popular selections were enthusiastically applauded. Both made brief acceptance speeches. The rock music resumed. And the residents began a slow, steady embarrassed dribble out of the Activity Room. The First Annual — and probably last —Haven Lake Sock Hop was over.

In retrospect, one must wonder how Adam and Geena let Ronny plunge so eagerly yet unwittingly into such a totally inappropriate activity.

Whether she was counseled or just learned from this failure, Ronny's next foray into musical affairs was a huge improvement.

It was an after supper soiree. A bar was set up in the Activity Room with an assortment of snacks and mixers for B.Y.O.B. A small live combo offered a delightful selection of oldies but goodies for a combination of name that tune and sing along. It was well attended by both residents and bottles. Now Ronny knows better what turns us out and turns us on!

No FUNNY MONEY was awarded for attendance at the Sock Hop. Much of it was earned for attendance at the musical soiree.

So let us return now to the subject of auctions where pockets are stuffed, envelopes bulge and sweaty fists overflow with bundles of FUNNY MONEY.

Many activities and special events have produced riches of FUNNY MONEY for many of us. Horse racing, conducted on a long sectioned-off table where horses are moved by throws of the dice, can be especially rewarding from both prize money and side bets. It is one of the most popular Haven Lake events. Poker also pays off handsomely.

But the real riches belong to the residents who participate in the most activities. It is as simple as that. Everyone knows who they are. Everyone knows how much they have — almost $2,000,000 for the wealthiest people in the latest auction. Everyone knows that the first choices of the best stuff will go to these wealthiest ones. But that puts absolutely no damper on the proceedings. FUNNY MONEY is printed with an expiration date that coincides with the auction date. Whatever is not spent at the auction becomes immediately null and void, scrap paper. You must spend it or lose it. The resultant bidding is wild and raucous.

At an auction early in our residency, long before the days of the millionaires, Fran and I had about $75,000 between us. That put us pretty much among the paupers. (It also said something about our level of participation in scheduled activities at that time.) But even then the bidding was frenetic. There were four bird feeders on display. I wanted one of them. Any one would do, so my strategy was fairly simple. I would let the wealthier folk bid as lavishly as they might care to on the first three feeders. I figured that by the time the fourth came up for bidding, other bird lovers in the room would have bought their feeder or spent themselves broke on other offerings. This is a very realistic expectation. The most popular offerings at every auction are several special dinners for a resident and seven guests to be served in the private dining room with a menu of the resident's choice. That choice is always Surf and Turf! The wealthiest go for these dinners with gusto and usually go broke to get one.

The auction of which I speak started at 2:00 PM. It was close to 4:00 PM when the third bird feeder was sold. It was time for me to make my move on the fourth feeder. In the meantime, another couple, having been outbid once too often, decided to leave. As they passed my chair I was handed all their FUNNY MONEY, about $120,000! I now had a total of some $190,000. That bird feeder was mine, for sure.

The bidding began. I let a few desultory bids go by. Some people can't hold back whether they want the item or not. Then I made my first bid, maybe $40,000 or $50,000. Judy topped me. This worried me. She and George had started with over $400,000. But they had been doing some buying. Surely they could not have as much FUNNY MONEY left as my untouched

$190,000. I confidently upped my bid by $20,000 just to let Judy know that I was serious and she might as well pull out. She upped me $20,000. I upped her another $20,000. Everyone in the room was laughing, cheering us on and loudly applauding each new bid. $190,000 was my last Hurrah. She went to $200,000 and I was done. I shook my fist at Judy and got the same right back.

It was now about 4:30 PM and people who had earlier spent their fortunes began to leave. Then Adam walked into the room and ordered auctioneer Ronny to cut it off. We were running seriously overtime. And there I sat with $190,000 in hand that would momentarily be worthless. But a number of items were still on the table. I could still squander my FUNNY MONEY on something, anything, to prevent a total loss. In desperation, I approached Ronny and said, "$190,000 for that box of assorted snacks."

"Sold!"

This is the kind of nonsense that makes the auctions great fun. If the Sock Hop was the pits, the auctions probably represent the pinnacle in respect to both programmed activities and special events at Haven Lake.

Which raises a momentous question: Are such goings-on a worthy way for the elderly to be spending their precious remaining time?

To get the answer to that question it must be recognized that "Scheduled" is the operative word for all of these occupations, be they programmed activities or special events. They have been conceived, planned, organized and are operated by management and/or residents. In other words, we want to do these things or we wouldn't be doing them. And we want to do them for the defined purpose of providing something to fill our latter years with some form of pleasure, satisfaction and sense of accomplishment. It is hard to make the case that any one of these activities and events is either a time-waster at best or wrong for us at worst. Indeed, the proof that every one of them fulfills its purpose is found in the level of participation each enjoys. Auctions thrive. Sock Hops expire.

Nevertheless, a proper judgment of how we elderly live our lives needs to recognize that planned occupations are definitely not the be-all and the end-all of our lives. By definition, we are enjoying *independent* living. We are not dependant upon others to determine how we spend our hours, our days and our years. We can and do think and act for ourselves.

Some residents, Ramona and Fred for instance, choose to engage in virtually no scheduled activities. It is apparent from mealtime conversations that they spend a great deal of time together watching sporting events on TV. Put the emphasis on together. They are equally avid sports enthusiasts. Who will question their preferences?

Steven brings a book with him to every meal. When waiting to be served, his head is bowed and his eyes are glued to the pages of that book laid in his lap. For some time, we thought he was sleeping and kidded him accordingly. He simply stopped reading long enough to wave the book at us, grin, and return to his perusing. He, too, is rarely seen at scheduled events, so we may assume, but cannot attest, that he spends most all of his time reading. Many would judge that an excellent use of his time.

Theresa is a walker. Oh, my, is Theresa a walker. One full course around the compound is one-quarter mile. Mary must complete at least six after most every meal.

All dog owners are walkers. Geena and her sheep dog. Janice and her dachshund. Gary and his border collie. My beautiful beagle, Maggie, and I complete the course four or more times a day. Carol and her chihuaha-doberman mix (the dog who caused my fall), do not walk much. He is too obstreperous for her to handle. (She has since found a more proper home for him.) Most all dogs at Haven Lake get along uncommonly well — just like the people.

Those fortunate enough to own and drive cars frequently take off from the community to enjoy outside, extracurricular activities. Many have nearby family with whom they frequently visit. It is well known that dining out is at the top of the list of such excursions. No matter that we have prepaid for all our meals, the urge to enjoy a change of taste and service is overwhelming. Drivers very often invite non-drivers to join them on these culinary outings in satisfaction of this universal urge. We do believe in "seniors serving seniors."

Shopping. Movies. Museums. Theater. Sight-seeing. Travel. All of these are known destinations for many residents who drive and are physically mobile and thus able to pursue at will an active life beyond the halls of Haven Lake. Some of these outside activities are also available to non-drivers through scheduled outings and group transportation provided by the community bus and driver.

So what do we old people do? It should be quite obvious that we do pretty much whatever we want to do, limited only by what we are able to do. What we do *not* want to do is listen to judgments about what we do. What we do not want is to be accused of "frittering" away our latter years in foolish activities. What we do not want is any inordinate worrying by others about the "significance" of our lives. What we most especially do not want is any preachments.

The elderly know, as only they can know, what activities they need and desire to fill their latter hours, days, years. And if they want something they are not getting, they do not hesitate to seek it out.

Like better food.

15.
Seared Basa with
Sesame Soy Citrus.

Food! First! Foremost! Finally! When in anyone's life has food not been a paramount factor? Enough food. Affordable food. Nutritious food. Delicious food. Fast food. Gourmet food. Ethnic food. Regional food. All are stars of our history and culture. Food production, food processing, food marketing, food services are major components of our national economy. Recipe books are best sellers. As babes we spit out our first taste of strained vegetables. As teenagers we binged on cheeseburgers, French fries and diet Coke. In the military we groused about "shit on a shingle." When we got married we compared our spouse's cooking to Mom's. The significance of food in everyone's life cannot be understated. And the fact that it plays a starring role in a retirement community such as Haven Lake should not be considered so unique. Except for one thing: At 80 years and older, we expect the culinary desires of a lifetime to be satisfied as never before.

This unnatural state of mind stems from one very simple, unique fact: The monthly rent we pay includes three meals a day. We have totally entrusted our taste buds and our stomachs to the care of the Haven Lake chefs. We have put our money where our mouth is! For that we feel the right to have a say in menu preparation. For that we feel the right to a certain standard of food quality and service. For that we feel the right to sit down to every meal with the expectation that it will be not only filling and nutritious, but enjoyable.

Without doubt, these same rights are being felt, these same tales are being told, in every other residence for the elderly, whatever its form, wherever its location.

Needless to say, we have put off the subject of food as long as possible. But given our doubts about the food in our first days in residence, who knew what might happen in the meantime? Maybe as the months passed there would come forth some smashing good news on the culinary front. The title of this chapter, for instance, cribbed from a menu a couple of months ago, was intended to launch another funny story a la mitzapuni soup. Who ever heard of seared basa with sesame soy citrus? But the laugh was on us. Basa, we learned on the day it was served, is a delicate, delicious variety of Far East fish. And sesame soy citrus is a scrumptious sauce that helped that fish melt in our mouths. Oops!

What was happening? Was Haven Lake food ascending to new heights of succulence? Well, not quite. But none could deny that it was getting better. How could it not? Criticism had been severe. Promises had been made. Some were kept. Some were not. But hope was in the air.

So now, if we are to show improvement over time it must be from a benchmark. Unfortunately, that benchmark must be this: Within a few months of the opening of Haven Lake, executive chef Jacob was in more hot water than the huge warming pans in his kitchen could hold. Residents were mumbling and grumbling among themselves. Yet we were all very new at this retirement community business and lacked the courage to speak up to management. As it happened, we were shocked into action.

In the community where Fran and I formerly lived, I belonged to a men's group that meets twice a month for breakfast. When we moved to Haven Lake, I was invited to keep coming to these enjoyable gatherings and did so. One such Monday morning less than a month after our move, a former neighbor asked me, "How are you enjoying that lousy food at Haven Lake?"

I was shocked. "What are you talking about?"

"C'mon! You know what I mean. I've eaten there a couple of times and I sure know it's lousy. And Lynda who's lived there for several months keeps asking us to take her out now and then just to get a decent meal."

I could make no rejoinder. I was embarrassed and deeply disturbed. If this kind of reputation was getting spread far and wide, Haven Lake was in serious trouble. Before I could decide if anything could or should be done about this sorry business, the fat hit the fire right there in the dining room. Our kitchen managed to savage two sacred holidays.

The first was St. Patrick's Day. The dinner menu offered corned beef and cabbage and boiled potatoes. What else would dare be served on this special day? Diners were salivating with anticipation for a dish that could not possibly be messed up.

Or could it? Adam came out of the kitchen that noon with coffee pot ready to pour but mumbling in a disgruntled tone. Those within earshot heard him say, "The cabbage smells like sauerkraut." This was not reassuring. Servers confirmed the impossible. The cabbage they served smelled and tasted like sauerkraut. On Saint Paddy's Day? Never! Yet the worst offense stared at us from the plate. The corned beef had been machine sliced cold-cut thin and looked more like the dried chipped beef ("shit on a shingle") of our military experience. Hard, tough, tasteless, it had obviously spent hours drying out in one of those warming pans and was now virtually inedible.

This happened when the first mitzapuny soup serving was still fresh in our minds. Though grossly dismayed, we were still reluctant to blow the whistle. Yet Adam himself had been witness to this disaster. We could hope that he would take action on his own.

Next came the roast turkey fiasco. The menu offering was clear and promising: Roast turkey with traditional dressing, mashed potatoes and gravy, cut green beans, cranberry sauce. Shades of Thanksgiving. Surely impossible to mess up. Guess again! Think of traditional roast turkey. Freshly sliced from the magnificently baked brown bird. Your choice of light or dark meat. A gravy boat from which to ladle as much as you wished on meat or dressing or potatoes. Now think of pulled barbecued pork. As we eyed our plates that day, it seemed certain that we erroneously had been served the latter. There was a small, rounded scoopful of pulled turkey, light and dark meat mixed together, gravy mixed in. There was a small, rounded scoopful of dry mashed potatoes. There was a small, rounded scoopful of dry dressing. Only the green beans, unscoopable, looked normal but were in fact overdone and mushy. Every diner in the room was stunned.

Seated at the next table, perhaps equally stunned by the sight on her own plate, Geena leaned over and asked me, "How is everything?"

I blew my top. "It is awful, as you can see. And in case you don't know it, the reputation of Haven Lake is going down the toilet and the flush water is coming right out of that kitchen!"

Her response was immediate. "Right after dinner, I want you to meet me and Adam and Jacob in the office."

Geena and I got there first and waited for Adam to fetch Jacob from the kitchen. I was like a crouched tiger ready to pounce but held off until all three could hear me out. The other two walked in and Adam started to say, "In defense of Jacob . . . "

Geena cut him off. "We will hear what John has to say first."

My tirade went something like this:

"Haven Lake is now our home. We burned our bridges behind us. We want and expect it to be the very best of its kind. I love and respect you, Geena and Adam, and believe you want Haven Lake to be the best. But you are scraping the bottom in respect to food quality and service and if you don't do something about that, you are going to get a reputation that will put you out of business."

After describing the corned beef and roast turkey fiascos, I added a few details about overcooked, mushy vegetables and dry, tasteless meats all left too long in warming pans. "Don't you have any concern about your own personal reputation," I challenged Jacob, "when you allow such awful stuff to leave your kitchen? For starters, get rid of the stupid ice cream scoops you are using for serving tools. Have you never heard about presentation?"

Adam interjected, "There are portion requirements from headquarters that must be followed."

"Fine! But remember that when you no longer have anyone here to serve. Eating three meals a day is the major activity of our lives in this place and if we can't take pleasure in it, how long do you think we will take it? We pay very well to live here and have every right to expect decent food service at the very least. You managers have an obligation to see that we get it. Yet it is obvious to all of us residents and should be equally obvious to you that the overriding goal in that kitchen is to make it easier, more convenient and cheaper for the chefs. The pleasure and satisfaction of the diners seem of little or no concern!"

Jacob sat in stony silence. When I finally ran out of gas, Geena quietly observed, "John is right about a number of things. I have observed them myself." And to me she said, "Thank you, John, for your honesty and the courage to speak up to us. We need residents like you to help us be as great as we really want to be. We hear you. We love you. We promise that we will take your complaints very seriously and that changes will be made. Now Adam and Jacob and I need to do some talking among ourselves."

I thanked them for hearing me out and left.

A management/resident meeting was held soon thereafter in which Geena acknowledged our general dissatisfaction with the food and promised definite improvement. She also expressed quite clearly her support for Jacob. Their relationship spanned a number of years and she was confident that he was the one best able to effect the necessary changes.

Our third chef, Carl, was hired shortly thereafter, reportedly to handle the growing number of residents and to help fulfill Geena and Adam's commitment to provide pleasing food service. His arrival led to a rumor that Jacob's replacement was now in place, but Geena's loyalty to him is unshakeable and he remains with us.

There began a slow, steady improvement in the quality of our food service. But that progress was far from smooth and a few more fiascos had yet to be endured. To the managers' credit, comment slips are always available in the dining room upon which we can record our complaints — or compliments when a good dish justifies. Geena assured us that every one of these is read and discussed with Jacob.

And so I continued to call a bad dish a bad dish!

In the wake of a few more sorry meals, I was compelled to write a letter to management detailing resident complaints tempered with some compliments where they were due. But the major thrust of this communication was to call into question what appeared to be Chef Jacob's "like it or leave it" attitude toward the food he prepared and the residents to whom it was served.

This venting of spleen produced a most remarkable aftermath. Readers will recall my failure to "buy" a bird feeder at the auction, as reported earlier. Now hear this:

Two days after I submitted that very critical letter, I sat in our living room before breakfast reading the morning newspaper when there came a tapping on the window. I looked up to see Jacob standing on the patio beckoning me to come out. When I did so, he said, "I heard that you couldn't buy a bird feeder you wanted, so I made one for you." Wherewith, he presented me with a clever concoction he had created out of PVC piping that formed, indeed, a very workable bird feeder, complete with the hardware, hooks and wiring needed to hang it as well as the feed to fill it.

Speechless for several moments, I finally muttered, "Thank you. Thank you so very much, Jacob. This is very thoughtful and I will use it with much pleasure."

"It's my pleasure," he replied. He showed me how to hang it. We shook hands and he departed — to go to his kitchen to serve us breakfast.

I did not ask and Geena did not tell me what had motivated Jacob's peace offering. I was happy to accept it and very ready to move on to whatever was yet to come. But in her own way she definitely let me know what Jacob's surprising gesture signified.

That same morning she made her usual boisterous entrance into the dining room wishing everyone a shouted "Good morning!" Proceeding from table to table as usual, hugging and kissing along the way, she finally made her way to my table. Grinning from ear to ear, she wrapped her arms around my shoulders, kissed me soundly on the lips and said, "I love you."

Such a display of affection was not unusual, but in this instance, the timing was pregnant with meaning. Jacob was not going to be dismissed. But he was going to be nicer to everyone. He was also going to match Geena's personal desire to make us happy with Haven Lake food. And I was still the courageous, respected whistleblower.

I would like to report that everything was peace, harmony, happiness and delicious eating forever after. I cannot. But after one more great disaster — involving our family gathered in Haven Lake's private dining room for a special occasion dinner — I wrote what I hoped would be my final letter of complaint. The table, I noted, was beautifully set with linens, china and crystal, the service was impeccable, but the food was a disaster!

I recommended the formation of a Culinary Committee of residents to personally monitor what was happening in the kitchen and make recommendations for needed changes.

Geena was just as upset by this unfortunate event as I was. "Could there possibly be a worse time for the kitchen to goof up so badly?" she asked. Adam was pleased to note that Carlos, the sous chef was on duty in the kitchen that day, not Jacob. Both pledged to maintain their determination to put such failures in the past.

My recommendation for a resident's culinary committee was studiously ignored — not surprising given the safety and sanitary regulations that prohibit a bunch of people from prowling around the kitchen from time to time. Nevertheless, I had made my point once again and food quality and service at Haven Lake finally began to show a slow but steady improvement.

The anxiety with which we had anticipated every meal gradually changed to curiosity. Were things really getting better? Would it last? Who should get the credit? In any case, we began to worry less about poorly prepared food and turned to frequent speculation about what exactly was being served.

Many incredible offerings were coming out of corporate headquarters on our daily menus. Hunter's Chicken. Golden Nugget Meatloaf. Sauerbraten with Gingersnap Sauce. Herb Crusted Pork Loin. Indian Summer Stew. Lemon Dill Chicken. Pork Medallions with Rosemary. English Trifle. Lazy Daisy Cake. Muffuletta Sandwich. Cranberry Meatballs. We began to wonder what the menu writers at headquarters were trying to achieve. Are these fancy menus a pretense? Or do they really believe that our dining experience can compete with fancy New York City or Los Angeles fancy restaurants? Are they confident that our chefs can deliver such succulence from their institutional kitchen? Have they considered that we might prefer good old fashioned home cooking, something more like a traditional offering from a roadside diner menu?

To their credit, our chefs now try to answer some of these questions. Jacob often tells us that he has changed a recipe or eliminated a menu item that does not meet the tastes or distastes or dietetic needs we have expressed in meetings with him. Mark tends to give us advance notice of the ingredients in unique recipes. Carlos gets earthy. "I never heard of it, so I just didn't make it." (He should have applied that reasoning to his English Trifle, which would cause Queen Elizabeth to turn over in her grave, as I readily told him.)

HOLD THE PHONE! Someone is tapping into my computer. These words — these very words — are being read by someone even as they are being written. Today, Sunday, the weekly menu was distributed at breakfast as usual. And on the back of that menu sheet — get this! — on the back of that sheet are listed half-a-dozen descriptions of menu items for the coming week! And get this, too. One of those descriptions reads as follows:

Baked Basa Provencal: Basa is a delicious, mild, white fleshed fish also known as White Ruffy. Provencal is a term referring to dishes prepared in the style of Provence, a region of France. Garlic, tomatoes and olive oil are the major trademark of Provencal cooking.

Please recall the heading for this chapter re. basa. Can this be coincidence? It seems impossible. But how can it be explained? One can only guess. The reformation of food quality and service at Haven Lake has been a long and involved process. Geena and Adam have been totally involved. Regional Manager Dennis has been heavily involved. We have had a few visits here from headquarters executives. They surely know what has been going on. No one has had to invade my computer. There has been a concerted effort to get this part of our lives done right. The new menu descriptions are simply one phase of a process initiated in response to our demands and expectations.

To complete the picture, it must be noted that there is always a second choice at both dinner and supper. These do not appear on the printed menu, but are announced by the chef before each meal. For the most part, second choices are more familiar, simpler dishes (diner-type fare) than the main menu item. The back of each daily menu also lists a selection of very simple dishes that are always available as substitutes for dinner or supper. These include such things as a fruit plate, choice of deli sandwiches, stuffed baked potato, garden salad plate, chicken breast, pastas and soup of the day. Thus we have adequate escape hatches if both the first and second choices give us pause. And those choices should not often puzzle us if we continue to be supplied with the new menu descriptions.

Finally, if none of these possibilities satisfies a particular taste, our servers will take a request for reasonable modification of a given menu item. "Leave off the fancy sauce, please," is a frequent special order. Veggies from the first and second choices can be interchanged. A choice of bread or bun or toast can be made for most sandwiches. Time was when such latitude was not offered and was, indeed, refused when requested. A request for toast instead of a waffle to go with scrambled eggs was once sharply denied by the server. "The toasting machine is not turned on." We got that one quickly handled; there is now a pop-up toaster in the kitchen in addition to the commercial model.

When all is said and done — and it mostly is — dependable conclusions can finally be made about this most crucial aspect of our life in Haven Lake, the dining experience.

Chef Jacob would have us believe that our kitchen does not serve institutional food. Our kitchen *does* serve institutional food. It can be no other way. There is no bank of cooks in our kitchen ready to prepare individual orders from a large restaurant-type menu. Only at breakfast are individual orders taken — for eggs. And service at that meal is consequently the slowest of the day.

Look into that kitchen before any mealtime and you will see tiers of prefilled plates under plastic covers stacked on counters waiting for servers to gather them up and pass them out to us. Look into that kitchen and you will see a row of large warming pans with steam gushing around them like geysers in Yellowstone National Park. Both of these are distinct markers of the institutional kitchen.

The warming pans were grossly misused in earlier days, probably for little more than the chef's convenience. Vegetables were cooked well ahead of mealtime and placed in these pans for so long they stewed into mush. Meats were sliced well ahead of time and placed in these pans long enough to turn them to leather. Fortunately, such destruction of good food and nutrition is happening much less often.

The final, inescapable truths are these:

Geena and Adam are making diligent efforts to keep their promises. They have listened to our complaints. They have challenged our chefs. Our chefs have responded to an appreciable extent. Like every other institution of its kind, Haven Lake serves good institutional food, probably a bit better than most. But it is not yet the best we hope it could be.

About 5% of the meals we are served make us want to dash to the kitchen and smother the chef of the day with compliments. About 5% of the meals we are served make us want to dash to the kitchen and dump them in the chef's lap. About 90% of the meals we are served are more or less satisfyingly edible. 100% of the meals we are served meet our nutritional needs and most certainly do not ever leave us hungry. And that's about as good as institutional food is ever going to get — anywhere!

It is a pleasure to be able to say, "Delicious meal, Jacob!" It will be a greater pleasure if and when we can have cause to say it again and again and again.

We must not leave the subject of food without kudos to those who serve it. Though they come and go, each one of them gets to know virtually all of us by first name. They know our preferences and dislikes. And though they have no real authority in the kitchen, they will go to bat for us to get some special request fulfilled if at all possible. And with eye-witness knowledge of what goes on in the kitchen (which we are forbidden to enter), they are known to offer sympathy when we voice our complaints.

When not serving in the dining room these servers are cleaning our apartments. All in all, they make a most positive contribution to our daily lives. We are not allowed to tip these people. But we can and do lavish them with praise

16.
Going bananas.

The hand was raised in the middle of a residents/managers meeting where Geena was presiding. When the woman was recognized she cried out, "I resent the fact that when bananas are passed out some people get them and other people don't get them. If bananas are to be distributed at all, every person should be treated equally and get a banana!"

The room was struck dumb. What was the woman talking about? Bananas! What bananas? When the truth finally dawned there was stunned disbelief.

Every two or three days, the kitchen receives a bulk delivery of bananas. Bunches are placed on a buffet table in the front of the dining room to be plucked and taken by anyone who wants a banana or two to put on cereal or take home for a snack. Long ago, sweet, smiling, silent Tina took it upon herself to dismantle these bunches and distribute the bananas. Well before any others arrive for breakfast she places one banana at each place setting —

well, at almost each place setting. It has long been known that she tends to miss a few. No one has ever presumed to embarrass her by asking why. Tina is simply another senior serving seniors. How fairly she does it has never been a matter of any great moment.

Until this day and this strident criticism.

When Geena got the gist of the complaint, she quietly suggested that no one should fault Tina. If she wished to do something thoughtful it was her privilege to do it in her own way.

Not so, continued the complainer. Bananas are being distributed. It is management's responsibility to see that it is done with equality for all.

Geena lost her cool. The woman got a dressing down. Geena got a dressing down in return. A voice from the back of the room (I can't help myself) cried out, "I can't believe we are wasting everyone's time with this silly discussion of bananas. Let's move on!"

"By all means," Geena agreed. But she was now steaming and had a bit more to say. She was hearing other unwanted things that had to be put to rest. Regional manager Dennis had reported to Geena that his recent private meeting with residents had produced much discussion of food quality and service, not all of it happy. A resident had then suggested to Geena that Dennis must have "slapped some wrists" because the food suddenly got better.

"I want everyone to get this very straight," Geena addressed the gathering through tight lips. "No one ever has to slap any wrists to get things done around here. Managing Haven Lake is our job. Adam and I are dedicated to that job. We do it to the very best of our ability. And it would help if we got a little more trust and respect from time to time from some of our residents!"

This received a burst of applause from residents and a much calmer "Thank you!" from Geena.

As I write, grandson John's admonition, "Keep it funny, Grampa," echoes in my head again. Well it might.

The next morning Geena and I met walking our dogs and had a howling good laugh about the bananas.

"That meeting was crazy," I said.

"Did I handle it okay?" she asked.

"Well," I chuckled, "you did get a bit carried away."

"Now you know why there is such a big turnover in community managers," she said.

I didn't know there was such a turnover let alone why. Is the job really that tough? Are the elderly really that nasty? Hoping for some answers to these questions, I have reviewed the published notes from past meetings of residents and managers.

There are four kinds of meetings. Residents with managers Geena and Adam. Residents with chef Jacob. Residents with regional manager Dennis. We have one or more of these meetings about once a month. And less frequently we meet with enrichment coordinator, Ronny.

In the meetings with Geena and Adam, Geena usually presides. The discussion is pretty much one way — from her to us. A repeated theme is the managers' dedication to our satisfaction, happiness and well being, delivered with such passion and emotion that it cannot be doubted. Upcoming activities might be announced. Rules, regulations and procedures are emphasized as might be necessary or timely. Residents are always invited to express their comments, questions, complaints and concerns. But by the time Geena gets through, there is usually little left to talk about — except the food service. Or maybe by then we are too timid to raise any other issues of greater import.

Meetings with chef Jacob are all about food, of course.

Meetings with Dennis have been mostly about food, despite the effort he always makes to cover a range of issues.

Meetings with Ronny are all about activities and the only ones where food is rarely mentioned.

It is easy to imagine managers getting fed up (no pun intended) with perpetual complaints about food. But giving up their jobs? Probably not. The bananas episode gives us a clue to the sort of thing that can really bug them. Geena truly lost her cool and her lecture about crabby people that followed may tell us why.

There exists without doubt an undercurrent of steady dissatisfaction that ripples throughout the community. It is endemic, rooted in two facts. (1) Retirement community living at its best is unnatural following as it does 80 or more years of life in normal homes and family relationships. (2) We are old, which at best is unnatural for all of us who once believed we were immortal. Under such circumstances, it is no wonder that we elderly tend to bitch a bit now and then. The unexpected, inexplicable outburst about bananas in open meeting was just one example. This sort of finicky gripe is usually whispered behind cupped hands or closed doors. It usually gets to managers as third-hand gossip. What managers get first-hand is a litany of complaints about the major aspects of our residency. The heating or air conditioning is unsatisfactory or not working right. The plumbing is stopped up. The tap water is too hot or not cold enough. The windows are dirty. The bus transportation is inconvenient or too slow. Or this capper: Someone left the water running and one, two or three apartments are flooded. The list is almost endless. Put all of this together and we can begin to see what can drive managers bananas. And the greater their dedication, the more frustrating they must find our picayune, often unwarranted and peculiar behavior.

As sure as it is true that our managers will never fully understand what it is like to grow old, it is equally true that we will never fully appreciate all the effort and sacrifices they regularly make on our behalf.

One of our particular, if not unusual, vagaries is a rumor mill that grinds out an occasional truth, many half truths and some downright errors. Among the rumors that filter through the ranks at Haven Lake is this one: John Doyle is Geena's "fair-haired" friend. I hope that is true. I know Geena respects honesty and listens to honest opinions.

Here's a rumor I have launched in turn: It could be that Geena and Adam are among the best managers in the business. And despite a raft of rumors to the contrary, they swear that they love Haven Lake and its residents, that it is their home as well as ours and that they will never leave us.

How do you like them bananas?

17.
Katie bar the door!

As the reader will have observed, these tales are progressive. They are being recorded much as they happen. And the unthinkable has now happened. Even as we have just finished lavishing praise upon them, management has been severely tested. And management has come up short.

Events of the past week are the sort we talk about in hushed tones. We ask "What if?" Then we mutter, "God forbid!" With fear and trepidation, we ponder what it would be like if some nasty contagion ever got loose within Haven Lake.

Now it has.

For a few days it was apparent to all residents that something unusual was going on. The regularly scheduled weekly apartment cleaning did not take place. We could get no explanation, just vague promises that it would eventually be done. Sarah, the delightful server who normally performed this function for us disappeared from the scene. So did our respected and greatly liked maintenance manager, Albert, right in the middle of a project he was working on.

Geena and Adam were conspicuous by their absence from the scene. Rumor had it that Geena had done some firing. Yet no one could or would tell us what had actually happened to these people or why.

Even as we pondered these mysteries, something much more ominous grabbed our attention: Emergency Medical vehicles were seen coming and leaving with a loaded gurney much too often.

Then we rose from bed one morning to find slipped under our apartment entrance door the following notice:

INITIAL LETTER TO RESIDENTS

DEAR RESIDENT:

WE ARE CURRENTLY EXPERIENCING WHAT APPEARS TO BE A NOROVIRUS THAT AFFECTS THE GASTROINTESTINAL SYSTEM. THE SYMPTOMS OF THE VIRUS ARE NAUSEA, DIARRHEA AND VOMITING. THE NUMBER OF RESIDENTS AND EMPLOYEES THAT HAVE REPORTED THESE SYMPTOMS IS VERY SMALL.

ALL RESIDENTS AND EMPLOYEES ARE ASKED TO PRACTICE CAREFUL HAND WASHING WITH WARM WATER AND SOAP (30 SECONDS) BEFORE EATING OR AFTER USING THE BATHROOM. WE ALSO RECOMMEND HAND SANITIZERS BE USED.

WE ARE ASKING RESIDENTS WHO HAVE

THESE SYMPTOMS: NOTIFY YOUR PRIMARY CARE
PHYSICIAN AND FAMILY.

  LET A MEMBER OF THE MANAGEMENT
TEAM KNOW IF YOU ARE EXPERIENCING ANY
SYMPTOMS. THIS WILL ALLOW US TO ASSIST YOU
IF FOR SOME REASON WE DO NOT SEE YOU IN
THE DINING ROOM.

  REMAIN IN YOUR APARTMENT AND
REQUEST MEAL TRAYS FOR ALL MEALS UNTIL YOU
ARE SYMPTOM-FREE FOR 48 HOURS.

  DO NOT ATTEND GROUP ACTIVITIES UNTIL
YOU ARE SYMPTOM FREE FOR 48 HOURS.

  REVIEW THE NOROVIRUS FACT SHEET.

  WE THANK YOU FOR YOUR COOPERATION.
PLEASE CALL THE OFFICE WITH ANY QUESTIONS.

  THANK YOU,

  THE MANAGEMENT TEAM

This was unwelcome news, to be sure. But it did seem to explain the disappearance of Sarah and Albert. They were undoubtedly among those taken ill. Beyond that, the description of the virus itself did not seem to be all that frightening.

Wrong! The message was erroneous! The truth was scary.

The notice clearly indicated that the dining room would be functioning as usual, albeit with proper care to be exercised on our part. Therefore, on that morning we went for breakfast as usual only to find the dining room dark, closed and empty. No one was there to tell us when, how or if breakfast — or any other meal — would be served.

There was no norovirus fact sheet provided for us to review and act upon. And bold red quarantine signs were seen posted at all main building outside entrance doors.

Confusion ruled.

Finally, about 9:30 that morning, there was a knocking at our apartment door and breakfast was served from a push cart by a server unrecognizable behind a medical face mask and wearing latex gloves. She had no answers for our questions about what was going on, except to advise us that the dining room would be closed until further notice.

This weird visitation was repeated for every meal every day thereafter, anywhere from one-half to one hour later than normal mealtimes. In response to repeated queries and complaints, the servers made it known that their carts offered no choices. Whatever the kitchen had sloshed into the Styrofoam boxes in which each meal was served was what we got, like it or not.

On day two of the emergency, an interim menu was slipped under our apartment doors. It confirmed what we already knew. No choices. Eat what you got or go hungry. Worse, it documented what we had already come to know. The kitchen was totally unaware of the nature of the crisis or, worse, just didn't care. To those who suffered vomiting and diarrhea, to those who were recovering from these maladies, to those who feared getting them, they served hamburgers and steak fries, hot dogs and mustard, chicken in gravy over noodles, sloppy Joes, sausage gravy and biscuits, jelly glazed kielbasa and sauerkraut. The trash bins on every floor were overfilled every day with Styrofoam boxes filled with food that was mostly inedible under the circumstances and often sickening on sight.

All the accolades accumulated by the Haven Lake chefs in the past six months were swept away in this one miserable week.

On the third day of the crisis an announcement came over the public address system. In effect, it advised that, just in case we had not noticed, all activities were cancelled. We were free to leave the premises if we wished, but were admonished to quit roaming the corridors lest we spread the contamination. Thus our only means of finding out what was going on, haphazard meetings and talks with our neighbors, was summarily prohibited. Except for an occasional leak from the servers who were our only regular contacts, we had no way of knowing who among our friends might be ill and no way of expressing our concern for them.

Throughout all of this, Geena and Adam remained in absentia. It was rumored that Geena was among those who were ill. Matthew and Amelia and part-timer managers Paul and Vivian were spotted now and then, but were answering no questions. Confined to our apartments, we had no idea what was going on in the realm of management. All in all, their communication with residents throughout this trying time was abysmal.

After a week of this misery, Geena's bubbling voice finally came over the PA system. It offered the "good news" that the end was in sight. Ill people were recovering. There were no new cases of the virus reported. The dining room would be reopened shortly. And then there would be a "celebratory feast" to thank us all for our wonderful cooperation and understanding.

Slipped under our apartment doors was this announcement:

DEAR RESIDENT:

GOOD MORNING. WE HAVE SOME GREAT NEWS. THE THREAT OF THE VIRUS SEEMS TO BE ENDING. THIS MORNING, FRIDAY, BEGINNING AT 8:00 AM, YOU MAY RESUME YOUR NORMAL ACTIVITIES, INCLUDING ATTENDING MEALS IN THE DINING ROOM.

IN HONOR OF YOUR PATIENCE, WE WILL CELEBRATE BY HAVING A SPECIAL MEAL. WE LOOK FORWARD TO SEEING YOU TOMORROW MORNING AND DINNER SUNDAY READY TO CELEBRATE.

REMEMBER WHEN ILL, PLEASE STAY IN YOUR APARTMENT AND LET US SERVE YOU MEALS UNTIL YOU ARE SYMPTOM-FREE FOR 48HOURS.

WE WANT TO THANK YOU FOR YOUR COOPERATION DURING THE NOROVIRUS OUTBREAK. THANK YOU, TOO, FOR THE MANY KIND WORDS OF APPRECIATION FOR THE STEPS TAKEN TO KEEP YOU SAFE AND HEALTHY.

WE DO APPRECIATE ALL OF YOU.

THE MANAGEMENT TEAM

At Sunday morning breakfast, Geena reappeared, made her usual boisterous entrance, bestowing hugs and huzzahs — no kisses — upon all in her path as she made her way from the back to the front of the dining room. She then took the microphone and informed us that she had, in fact, been sick, but with bronchial pneumonia, not the norovirus. She deeply regretted that she had not been able to personally manage the crisis. Glad to be back, she was anticipating the noontime celebration to come.

At that Sunday dinner the real damage control began.

Chef Jacob announced that the main course was to be surf and turf — sliced seared beef and lobster — but with a strange twist. The lobster, "lots of it," he said, was being served in a macaroni and cheese casserole! Old timers in the dining room exchanged knowing glances. Be the food good or bad, coming from our chefs it would surely be weird. But the beef was delicious and the macaroni, cheese and lobster combo was surprisingly edible. After dinner, Geena solicited and got a round of applause for Jacob.

She then offered a praise-the-Lord speech for our deliverance from the plague, thanked us for our patience and cooperation — and launched her main defensive thrust:

"In circumstances like this," she said, "the menu is prescribed by corporate headquarters. So if you didn't like the food you were served in your apartments, blame them, not our chefs."

Few of us were mollified by this disclaimer. Any dietary "expert" in headquarters responsible for this week's menu ought to be fired. Our chefs have boasted about the latitude they have in menu fulfillment. This was surely the time to overrule any thoughtless dictates and replace them with more appropriate fare!

Adam then took the microphone to give us his "two cents worth." He wanted us to know that only eleven people had suffered from the virus. This was far fewer than recorded for any other community contaminations the company had ever experienced in the past. He was sure that the prompt closing down of the dining room and cancellation of all activities had contained the malady and was the right thing to do. With this informative and significant notice, the first of its kind in a week, the celebration was over.

The total effect upon the community and its residents and managers was not revealed until the next open meeting of managers and residents. Yes, it was agreed that the virus had been controlled and in good time. But the dissatisfactions recorded here — dismal communication and unpalatable food — were, surprisingly, simply not expressed by any residents. Thankful for that, no doubt, management also ignored the subject. Consequently, we learned nothing about any lessons they or we might have learned for future guidance and implementation in such an emergency.

A couple of us discussed how weird this resident silence seemed to be and pondered what it could mean. Significant answers are elusive. Just questions remain. Is it possible that among all the ills, worries and sufferings endured by the elderly, this brief virus attack was relatively insignificant? Is it possible that management and staff are really not qualified to properly deal with such a crisis? Is this something we just don't want to think about? Or was that week — and the possibility of an even worse repeat — so scary that we just don't want to talk about it?

The latter question could be closest to the truth. Consider the following exchange, of which some version is too often heard in the halls of Haven Lake.

"How are you?"

"I'm fine."

"Yes, I know. But how *are* you?"

"I told you, I'm fine."

"Of course you are. And when they go to close the lid on your coffin, you will sit up and say, 'I'm fine.'"

With such badinage do we avoid the truly dismal realities of the aging process.

At that meeting, we did learn that Sarah and Albert had not been ill with the virus. She had been let go. He had quit. No reasons were given. Aha! Now we had something to gossip about that would help take our minds off the more dire facts of community life.

18.
Esoterica.

Viral epidemics aside, these tales about the elderly have dealt with a lot of seeming nonsense. What we eat. What kind of games we play. FUNNY MONEY. Silly auctions. Inconsequential bruises. Petty irritations. This might suggest that life in the retirement community is a pathetic, purposeless, culturally impoverished existence. Any such conclusion would be very wrong. We need to explore the many aspects of our existence that ennoble our latter days.

Despite what you have read here, "Man does not live by bread alone." Just as the Bible (Matthew & Luke 4:4) settles that score, a great poet suggests what else might be more important in our lives, "Beauty is truth, truth beauty. That is all ye know on earth and all ye need to know." (John Keats, "Ode to a Grecian Urn.") Keats died 190 years ago at just age 26, but his words have touched all generations and all ages to this day. We cannot be ill advised to explore beauty and truth as the most pertinent aspects of life at

Haven Lake that lift it out of the mundane and onto some higher plane.

"Beauty is truth." I readily return to our first interpersonal experience — meeting Ramona and Fred in the dining room. You will recall that they reminded us of the painting, "American Gothic" by Grant Wood. With that image in mind, you might wish to join me in the suspicion that Ramona and our resident hair dresser do not schedule too many sessions together. And maybe Ramona has heard of Maybelline, though I doubt the acquaintance remains very active today. Yet I tell you this with all certainty: Ramona is beautiful! Gently, peacefully, quietly, gracefully beautiful. She sets the standard within our community for that old axiom "beauty is more than skin deep."

At over 80, skin deep beauty is hard to find. A typical beauty contest held in Haven Lake would, of course, find no qualifiers. But if you set Ramona as the standard of womanly beauty, very many of the Haven Lake women could take the stage with confidence.

Beauty is not restricted to the women. Many of our beautiful people are men. Ramona's Fred is one of them, an example of the devoted husband, for sure, but equally matching in character.

Remember Steven the reader? He found an added avocation when Ethan, a new resident confined to a wheelchair, became his next door neighbor. Steven soon began to push that wheelchair wherever his neighbor needed to go, book still ever in hand. Beautiful!

But as soon as Ethan became acclimated to his surroundings, began to make friends and, yes, began to get involved in some activities, he said to Steven, "Thanks, but no thanks. I can get around now quite well on my own." Beautiful!

Dan and Anne have become very frequent table partners for Fran and me and very dear friends. While Anne maintains her greatly admired regal demeanor, Dan has won our love in turn with innumerable demonstrations of his gentle, loving, understanding, Christian nature. Complaints may circulate, rumors may abound, but Dan has nothing but kind words for all people and a peacemaking attitude towards all conflicts. Beautiful!

Beautiful people we've got.

Beautiful surroundings we've also got, both inside and out.

A prime reason repeatedly stated by many residents for choosing Haven Lake is its ambience. The interior is open, airy, well lighted, handsomely furnished and decorated. The first impression upon walking through the front door is pleasing and welcoming in every respect. And that feeling is not lost as you tour from room to room, corridor to corridor, floor to floor. You never feel crowded. Nothing you experience is ever dingy or dark or depressing. It is truly a place of beauty where it is easy to feel happy.

The exterior is equally inspiring. We should be able to eat our landscaping! It is that superb. From the lavishly planted entry way, take the quarter-mile walk around the building and you will see nothing that does not please the eye. Every square yard of planting bed is thickly mulched and weed-free. Every flowering shrub, bush and tree — there are literally hundreds — is healthy and thriving. If not, it is speedily replaced. Wide walkways with graded curbs enable every resident to circumnavigate the property with ease regardless of mobility problems. This is truly a garden of beauty that lifts the spirit.

Alongside the front driveway a small pond is home to one of the largest snapping turtles any of us has ever seen. Now and then this astonishing beastie waddles up the hillside to the road to give us a closer look at his gaping jaws. On the far side of the building, a short path through the woods leads to a beautiful small lake that delights the eye and invites a walk along its banks from end to end. A family of beavers makes its home here and the work of their gnawing teeth is everywhere to be seen. Fallen saplings, chewed off by the beavers, appear now and then only to soon disappear as they are devoured by the pack. Both sunrise and sunset turn the lake into dazzling displays of color.

Our beloved beagle, Maggie, takes great delight in our frequent walks through the woods along the lake, her busy nose exploring every scent along the way. Beautiful times.

It is unfortunate that some handicapped residents are unable to explore this lovely lake. It is astonishing that others say they have never thought to do so. But neither fact lessens its beauty and truth.

Truth be told, the lake does not belong to Haven Lake but falls within the property of an adjoining charter school. A security guard from the school greets us now and then, knows us as harmless old coots, and assures us that we are always most welcome to enjoy his lake.

"Truth beauty." Elderly people seldom stretch the truth. They rarely need to. Virtually all the reasons for prevarication have been swept from our lives by the evolution from a work-a-day world to retirement status. We fibbed as kids to get out of chores and homework. We fibbed as teenagers to get a date or get out of a date. We fibbed to get our girlfriends to accept our marriage proposal. We fibbed to our wives when we had to stay out late after work. We fibbed to get ahead in our careers. We fibbed to the boss when we took a day off. We fibbed on our income tax returns. The list goes on and on. Fibbing in our prior life was a necessary and accepted means of survival. Today we just fib to our doctors about taking our medications.

All the goals we once pursued that tested our honesty have vanished. We no longer have much purpose to shade the truth. In old age, truth takes on a meaning that it seldom had in all our previous years. The truth is that our health is waning. The truth is that our minds are wandering. The truth is that our legs are unsteady. The truth is that our days are numbered. The truth is that friendships are more precious than ever. The truth is that each day is an incredible gift to be enjoyed to the fullest. For many of us the greatest truth at this age might be something we probably cared too little about in years gone by. And that is that God loves us.

It will be difficult for those who have not experienced these elderly facts of life to understand that there can be beauty in such formidable truths. But if you want to try, imagine yourself in our place and consider this: We have committed ourselves to a retirement community just because we must and do accept all the truths enumerated above. And taken as one or taken as all, they give us proof that we are *not* immortal as we thought we were most of our lives. We are not going to live forever. Try to think of that revelation as we do. Now we can relax. Now we can get out of the worldly rat race. Now we can allow ourselves to appreciate and enjoy that incredible gift of another day. Now we can ponder if we so desire what comes at the end of life. Now we can prepare ourselves as we see fit to face that inevitability. Or we can conclude that when the end does come it will be the end of all. Whatever! We are released from all worldly concerns. We are freed to exercise our intellect and free will, humanity's unique capabilities, to do no more than deal with our newly recognized mortality. Nothing could be more purposeful. Nothing could be more significant. Nothing at our ages could give us a greater sense of beautiful equanimity.

But another truth about the elderly must be confessed: We tend to be quite naïve about the significant role we play in general society. Our daughter, Ginny, recently said to me, "Your grandson, John, latches on to your every word and action." How scary is that? What kind of responsibility is that to bear? And I think about all the people in Haven Lake and wonder how many are aware of such burdens upon their behavior, their words and their example.

Certainly, children and grandchildren are often seen in the community as visitors. Signs of affection are displayed. Proud introductions are made. But are the impressions we make upon our offspring by these brief encounters good or bad? Are they moved by the truth and beauty of which we speak here? Not likely. They see very little of it. More likely, they see the nonsense that is much more obvious most of the time.

It is a simple, if regrettable fact, that a retirement community is not an environment from which to project an example of great personal accomplishment in the making. Whatever we may have achieved in years gone by counts for little now. The opportunity, perhaps the obligation, we have now as never before, is to demonstrate to succeeding generations the courage, the strength, the perseverance required of us simply to grow old gracefully. It could be the most important, most inspirational lesson they could ever learn from us.

There may be a lot of nonsense in our lives, but be assured that there is also beauty and truth.

19.
Tale's End.

We have chosen to spend the last days of our lives in an independent living retirement community. At the time of that choice, logic and good advice seemed sufficiently justifying. Now we are learning whether it was a very good decision or maybe terribly wrong. Clues are found in what we see happening in our daily lives.

To date, voluntary departures from Haven Lake since it opened have numbered only five. Two of them were gentlemen who never did seem well at home. They kept much to themselves. And one day they were gone. Clearly, these were people giving it a try. We will never know exactly why they decided to leave. The third man was unhappy from the start. "I was put here by my sons for their own convenience," he told anyone who would listen. (As noted earlier, this is *not* a common attitude.) He didn't like that he had to smoke his pipe outside on his patio. He definitely didn't like the food. "I can cook for myself better than that." He had kept his old home in case he wanted to go back and so he did. The fourth departure was a husband and wife couple for whom financial expectations did not materialize. They could no longer afford Haven Lake and have moved to a nearby apartment. The fifth occasion for departure was the sort we don't like to think about. Beautiful Brenda could no longer pursue an independent lifestyle. She is now well placed in a total care facility.

The rest of us are learning to accept our new life with a variety of feelings. It is positively gleeful for some. "I really don't mind if the food is not great. I did not have to cook it!" Others are just willing. "I sure don't miss all the problems of a big house." Reluctance is not uncommon. "My family thinks this is best for me." For most it is simply inevitable. "I just couldn't manage on my own anymore." Few of us will ever say that we prefer to be here rather than anywhere else. We are here because we are old and need to be here. And that is a situation loaded with uncertainties.

What if we get sick? This possibility does not seem to be at the top of our list of concerns. Sickness is something we have known since we had chicken pox at age five. We went to bed; Mom took care of us. Other times we went to the hospital where a sweet nurse gave us loving care. In either case, we got well. Sicknesses are a familiar, if pesky, part of life, but not all that frightening. Indeed, our managers advise us, "If you get sick, please just stay in your apartment so as not to infect others. We will make sure that you get fed while you recover."

But in less than a year of residency, events have forewarned us of much more drastic uncertainties. Beautiful Brenda fell just once too often. More often than we like to witness, one of us gets whisked out of here by ambulance to the hospital, most often to the emergency room. Someone has fallen. Someone has respiratory difficulty. Someone's heart has been acting up. Someone has fainting spells. Name your malady, we are likely candidates. Fortunately, most who have left by ambulance have returned within a short time sufficiently recovered to resume our kind of independent living. But we all know all too well that this will not always be the case.

What if we become disabled, physically or mentally? An entire chapter of this book has been devoted to the mobility problems endured by the elderly. You already know how creatively, capably and kindly they are managed in Haven Lake. But it is one thing to have a disability; it is quite another thing to be disabled. Another chapter has delineated the requirements for admittance to and the reasons for dismissal from an independent living retirement community. We have all read and signed the documents that govern these stipulations. In simple, stark truth, we know that if we become totally disabled, physically or mentally, we are out of here! That was a gamble we took when we came here. If we are smart, we have also explored and specified with loved ones or other caretakers what happens if we lose that gamble. Some of those possibilities have also been discussed earlier.

What if we become terminally ill? We have — or should have — properly executed documents that address this contingency. First, a living will that specifies what kind of care we wish to receive or *not* to receive if we are terminally ill. Second, a medical power of attorney that gives some loved and trusted person the legal power to enforce our living will. Ronny has invited specialists in this field to visit and advise us and serve us, if need be. It is not an infrequent subject for discussion among us.

Surprisingly — or maybe not so surprisingly in view of the beauty and truth we enjoy — one hears very little said about the fear of dying. The almost inevitable conclusion to such a discussion is something like this: "I've lived a long and good life. I can no longer undo anything I might have done wrong. There is not a lot more of any significance that I can add to it. So what can be so bad about dying and leaving this life?"

We elderly know as no others can know it the inexorable march of time. We remember that four years of high school was an eternity. We still cringe from the recollection of the never-ending suffering of three-plus years of military service in World War II. We waited forever to get that promised promotion, that overdue raise in pay. Our eligibility for Social Security was forever over the horizon. But now the years sweep by so swiftly that we lose track of our own birthdays. We know we have no time to fret and worry about the inevitable consequence of growing old. Every day is precious. Every day we know the joy to be found in just being alive.

Of course, all our lives we have known and seen that death is not reserved for the elderly. It can and does strike instantly, at any time, at any place, at any age. Yet that knowledge simply reaffirms how incredibly fortunate we are to have come this far.

The single greatest distinction between the young and the elderly could be the relative awareness of mortality. Like the rest of mankind, we too thought we would never die — until we passed the age of eighty. Now the thought of death is our constant companion. We do not dwell on it. We do not sweat about it.

We rarely discuss it. And, for the most part, we do not fear it. We just know and accept that it is going to happen — probably sooner than later. Those of us who profess a religious persuasion (and none have been heard to say that they do not) view death with an added sense of peace born of a belief in God's love, forgiveness and promise of eternal life.

As I approach 90 years and, inevitably, my own tale's end, a familiar prayer often comes to mind. It is that first prayer most of us learned from our mothers as toddlers at the beginning of this life. It may be more timely now than it ever was then.

Now I lay me down to sleep,

I pray the Lord my soul to keep.

If I should die before I wake,

I pray the Lord my soul to take.

Amen.

Afterword

Even as this book is being written, life goes on at Haven Lake and changes are forever taking place. Some of these have been significant — significant enough to bring them to the attention of our readers who might otherwise be left wondering. To wit:

Former assistant managers Tyler and Caralee have returned to this area. They are now the head managers of a sister community in northeast Charlotte. They are now in possession, by the way, of the Wii bowling trophy for which regular competitions are held between Haven Lake and two other sister communities in this area. We here are dedicated to wining it back — having failed three times before!

Former assistant managers Matthew and Amelia have left this area. They are now head managers of a sister community in South Carolina.

The reputation of Haven Lake as a training ground for future managers remains intact and unchallenged.

The new assistant managers who then came aboard served only a couple of months before health problems forced their resignation. Geena is now seeking their replacements.

Corey , a recently discharged Marine and new husband and father is now our Maintenance Manager. Though not as ebullient as Albert, he is every bit as competent.

"Seniors Serving Society" is now an active program initiated by Ronny. As the name of this activity implies, it entails forays into the world outside of Haven Lake. Thus only the hale and hearty are able to participate. But the few who do are most enthusiastic and happy to help fulfill this corporate goal.

Mitzapuny soup continues to appear on our menus!

Appendix:

Letters to management about food service.

I hope to have shown that courage and candor are the keys to good relations with community managers. As capable and conscientious as they might be, managers never totally know what is going on in the community, good or bad. They want to hear from their residents. If you want them to do well by you, you will never fail to tell them the truth, as I did in these letters. (It was the first letter that precipitated chef Jacob's peace offering of a hand-made bird feeder.)

July 1, 2009

Dear Geena and Adam:

Attached are copies of my latest and final commentaries on the Haven Lake dining experience. I have followed your repeated instructions to freely express any complaints. I have believed your repeated promises of total dedication to resident satisfaction. But mine has been a voice crying in the wilderness.

I should have seen the futility when chef Jacob deeply insulted you before the entire community without reprimand. Remember? Or did you not know? The day after you instructed him to tone down his menu presentations, he delivered before the entire community a sarcastic, self-pitying replay of your instructions. We did not like him before. That day we liked him much less. To this day, he delivers each menu announcement with unveiled, egotistical barbs about your unwanted restrictions on his thespian powers.

I knew my personal battle was lost when Jacob delivered his vociferous speech -- clearly directed at me -- after Saturday supper, June 27. With no sense of any shortcomings on his part, with no fear of censure from you, he virtually directed all of us to like it or lump it.

Your stance in this conflict seems clearly stated in the final lines of the Notes from the Chef's Meeting, June 17, 2009. "The residents enjoy the food and the great job Jacob and his staff are doing for them." (Where does that come from? Conduct a survey!)

I don't know how many other residents have expressed their displeasure with the food service. But following management instructions to "mingle in the dining room," we have done much of that lately. And I assure you, dissatisfaction is deep and widespread. Others might be too shy, reluctant or fearful to express their disappointments, but be certain that fault findings are many and real. You need to fear for the reputation of your community.

Yes, we get sufficient sustenance to maintain our health. But the dining pleasure we rightfully expect three times a day is rare. Every menu sheet, every meal is greeted with apprehension or forced jokes about what strange concoction or ruined good food might next be placed before us. Thank God for the social pleasure enjoyed at mealtime that supersedes the poor quality of the food.

I know it is not within your will to replace Jacob, and that has never been requested. But I hope it is within your power to change

125

his attitude and cooking methods, at least — and do it before this persistent problem gets to Regional Manager Dennis and beyond, a possibility some are now discussing.

In the meantime, we will concentrate on the joy we find in the delightful people with whom we share this otherwise wonderful place.

Sincerely yours,

John Doyle

Attached to that letter was this listing of my previous complaints:

DINNER – JUNE 25

The stewed okra and tomatoes were the most disgusting looking and slimy tasting stuff we have ever seen served on a food plate. The okra was overcooked into mush, with seeds floating around in it looking like a batch of mealy bugs. The tomatoes were almost too few to be seen let alone tasted. A good chef would be ashamed to serve such an abomination!

DINNER – Saturday, June 27

The hot dog and coleslaw were very good. I chose them as the least likely to get messed up. GOOD CHOICE, because the hamburger served to a dining partner looked like a hunk of charcoal that might have been used to cook it. It was, in fact, so burned dry and hard that it could not be cut with a knife and fork – let alone eaten as a hamburger sandwich. It was left uneaten, of course. Is this a fair question: How does something so obviously BAD ever manage to leave a kitchen where the chef puts his reputation on the line with every meal?

SUPPER – Saturday, June 27

Fair is fair! The bacon, lettuce and tomato sandwich was great! So was the watermelon. Is this a fair question: Is a BLT just something the chef can't mess up?

More fair! The lamb stew alternative for supper, Thursday, June 25 was excellent! Is this a fair question: Can it be so difficult to consistently serve such quality?

DINNER – Sunday, June 28

I ate all of it but enjoyed little. As usual, good ham and good roast beef were sliced early and left sitting in a warming pan long enough to turn them dry and quite tasteless. At the same time, the cauliflower au gratin was over-cooked into a watery slush.

SUPPER – Sunday, June 28

*Chef Jacob's little speech this evening about how much he **doesn't** get paid shows again how totally out of touch he is with the reality of the situation. It had absolutely no bearing upon any thing that has been said about his performance. It reveals once again a totally self-centered, defensive attitude towards any criticism. When displeased with any serving, we are now instructed by him to raise a hand like a grade school child whereupon a manager on duty will respond and offer to replace the offending item. With what? More of the same?*

John

July 25, 2009

Dear Geena and Adam:

Once again, I fear for the reputation of the community.

My younger sister from Louisville, Sister Mary Ellen, visited here this weekend. I invited her and the whole Charlotte family, seven in all, to "enjoy" dinner in the guest dining room this noon. The setting was elegant, thanks to Amelia. The service was excellent, thanks to Channing, Amelia and Matthew.

The food was a gross embarrassment! Badly overdone chopped sirloin was dry, hard and tasteless. In contrast, the potato gratin was so grossly underdone that the slices could be cut only by knife. The diners were kind enough to remain speechless. I was forced to offer an apology.

I learned later that some residents were served nicely done, delicious chopped sirloin. This only compounds the problem and begs two questions that I have often asked: 1. If it can be done right some of the time, why not all of the time? 2. Doesn't anyone check the quality of servings before they leave the kitchen?

I truly believe you are dedicated to the solution of the food quality problem. But I have also come to believe that there can be no lasting solution until these questions can be answered and proper remedial action taken. And I also believe that it is very difficult for just the two of you – or all the managers together -- to get this done. I want to offer help.

Specifically, I want to recommend the formation of a Culinary Committee of residents. I believe many would be eager to join. The committee's assignment would be very simple – make appointments and prepare a schedule for residents to personally monitor what is happening in the kitchen. This might be the only way to get the information that is needed to make meaningful, lasting changes.

If you agree that this idea has any merit, I'd like to discuss details with you and get started to get it done.

I want so very much to write a happy ending to my new book!

Sincerely,

John